From Workhouse to Prison to ....
the Titanic ?

Think then you are TO-DAY what YESTERDAY
You were --- TO-MORROW you shall not be less
(Omar Khayyam)

~~~~~~~~~~~~~

Dinah Burnett

~~~~~~~~~~~~~~

For my mother -
and all those she helped who have stood by her
and abided by her wishes

British Library Cataloguing in Publication Data
Title: *From Workhouse to Prison to .... the Titanic ?*
ISBN 0 9537288 0 3
A catalogue record of this book is available
from the British Library

Printed in the United Kingdom by
Unwin Brothers Limited
Old Woking
Surrey GU22 9LH

Published by Dinah Burnett
All enquiries/contact in relation to this publication
should be made via - www.dinahburnett.co.uk

Contents

1. The Titanic and my Mother   5

2. Accusations and the Accuser   7

3. In Search of the Truth   14

4. The Story of Alice Cleaver   17

5. To London and Back   39

6. Let the Truth Speak for Itself   45

7. Summing Up - The Weight of Evidence   65

8. The Lesser Charges:-   72
    a.   Inexperience ?   73
    b.   Leaving the Titanic   76
    c.   The Carpathia to New York   89
    d.   A False Identity ?   100
    e.   Appearances can be Deceptive   107
    f.   The 1940's and "Mrs. Gray"   113

9. Deliberation and Verdict   117

10. The Final Judgement   119

~~~~~~~

Acknowledgements & Bibliography   125

1

The Titanic and my Mother

I don't remember when I first became aware that my mother was a *Titanic* survivor, I think I must have always known. It was just an accepted fact in the family, no fuss was made, occasionally something would happen and the subject would crop up, but with a child's instinct it was never a topic I myself raised. Even at a young age I was aware of the pain my mother suffered from her memories of that terrible tragedy, and how she never forgot those who lost their lives. Like so many involved in a traumatic event in their young years only many years later was she able to talk about it more freely.

Throughout her life she was pestered by journalists and students, who tracked her down, wanting to know her experiences. To them it was just a story, and they could not imagine the pain of someone reliving the nightmare.

Despite all this my mother retained her anonymity, at least as far as the general public were concerned, after all she was just one of many servants travelling on the *Titanic*, one of many who were of so little importance they were known only by their positions, not their names.

The public, informed by sensationalist newspapers of the day, had followed the stories of Captain Smith, Bruce Ismay, the

Astors, Duff Gordon and countless others, but who was Nurse Cleaver ? Amongst the hundreds of stories that appeared there was brief reference made to the nurse who saved the Allison baby - her charge. There were many brave and heroic acts that night, and knowing my mother as I did I would have expected no less than total dedication to her duty, putting others before herself.

I'm sure she expected interest in the *Titanic* to decline over the years, to be renewed only by anniversaries and the like. She would never have believed that so many years after the disaster the curse of the *Titanic* would be visited on those she left behind.

To me the very name *Titanic* was synonymous with senseless loss of life and suffering, not a subject on which I ever wished to dwell. If someone had suggested eighteen months ago I would be writing *any* book I should have dismissed it, if they'd said it was to be connected with the *Titanic* I would have thought them mad. But survivor Washington Dodge was so disturbed by interviews in the press attributed to him and his wife, when no such interviews had taken place, that in the May of 1912 he made an address to the Commonwealth Club in San Francisco, which was later published. I am so horrified by what has appeared about my mother in books, films and on the internet that I too feel compelled, like others before me, to set the record straight.

2

Accusations and the Accuser

In the summer of 1998 it came as a tremendous shock to learn of the accusations being levelled against my mother, by none other than the Historian of the Titanic Historical Society (based in Massachusetts) - Mr Donald Lynch. They came in the form of a book, *Titanic: An Illustrated History*, published in the UK by Hodder & Stoughton/Madison Press. Little as I wish to bring publicity to this book, which in view of the terrible things it says about her I feel it does not deserve, it cannot be ignored.

I, and the rest of my mother's family therefore found ourselves in the sort of situation which none of us could possibly have imagined.

~~~~~

As you read my book think of your own mother, grandmother and those you still grieve for, and realise then that their reputations whilst they are alive and able to speak for themselves are protected, at least to some extent, by recourse to law. After they are dead, no matter in what regard they are held and how much they are cared for, there is nothing to protect them from assault on their character - not even the truth itself.

According to Mr Lynch my mother, Nurse Cleaver, was guilty of:-

Child Murder

Obtaining Employment as a Nursemaid by Deception

Responsibility for Death of a Family

Keeping Control of a Baby in an Attempt to Afford herself Protection and Gain Financial Advantage

Concealing her True Identity to Hide her Past

Being of an Unprepossessing Appearance

Taking Part in Attempted Extortion

Most of these charges are stated outright, some are by a degree of implication, but nevertheless the reader is made fully aware of all of these accusations.

Below is a summary of each charge Mr Lynch makes against Nurse Cleaver:-

She was a convicted child murderer i.e. she had murdered her own illegitimate son in 1909, been tried and convicted but later released.

~~~~~

She gained employment as a children's nursemaid with the Allison family by deception i.e. she did not make her employers aware of her past, and was not an experienced nursemaid.

~~~~~

She was responsible for the Allison family going to their deaths on board the *Titanic* i.e. she took baby Trevor without his mother's consent. Mrs Allison, unaware of what had happened to him, would not leave the *Titanic*. The Allisons and their little girl all perished.

~~~~~

She maintained sole control of the baby whilst on board the rescue ship the SS *Carpathia*, for reasons other than the purely professional ones of a nursemaid's duty towards her charge i.e. to benefit herself in a mercenary way, and also gain some kind of unexplained protection.

~~~~~

She concealed her real identity to hide her past i.e. when the *Carpathia* reached New York she deliberately supplied waiting reporters with a false name.

~~~~~

She was of an unprepossessing appearance i.e. her picture had to be enhanced before it could be shown because it would not correspond with the image of how the baby's nurse and saviour ought to look.

~~~~~

She took part in attempted extortion in North America in the 1940's i.e. she aided and abetted Lorraine Kramer in claiming to be Lorraine Allison by supplying her with Allison family memories.

The overall picture he paints of Nurse Alice Cleaver is of a woman *"nervous yet excited"*, already in the employment of the Allison family from Montreal, and first introduced to us on board the RMS *Titanic* the morning of her departure from Southampton, 10th April 1912. The prospect of such lavishness as offered by the *Titanic* and undertaking the voyage itself is, we are told, something she could never have envisaged.

Supposedly, Nurse Cleaver had been *"hired in haste"* by Mrs Allison as nursemaid for her two children (Lorraine and baby Trevor), having hidden not only her inexperience in this role, which her employer was now beginning to discover, but also a much darker aspect of her past -

She was a Convicted Child Murderer -

having in 1909 murdered her own illegitimate child, a baby boy, by throwing him from a railway carriage to be found by men working on the line the following day. She proclaimed her innocence, stating her child had been handed to a *"Mrs. Gray"* to be placed in a north London orphanage, but neither could be located. She was found guilty of this crime but the jury taking into account her situation, following desertion by the father of her baby, recommended leniency and she was ultimately released.

This then is apparently the background for Nurse Cleaver taking employment with the Allison family in 1912 on the *Titanic,* in order to make a fresh start in Canada away from her past. Her past, however, were it discovered, would be the very thing to ruin these plans.

We next meet up with Nurse Cleaver shortly after the fateful collision of the *Titanic* with the iceberg - the night of 14th/15th April. The Allison's maid, Sarah Daniels, had twice attempted to alert the family to her misgivings without success, only engaging Mr Allison's anger. She therefore dressed, and getting no further with the nurse, who wouldn't wake the baby, left their staterooms. On reaching the deck, despite wishing to return to warn the family, her protestations were swept aside and she was placed in a lifeboat.

Eventually Mr Allison stirred, became aware something was wrong and went to find out. Mrs Allison was distraught, and the nurse had to help her dress and otherwise assist her, but when a steward ordered them to leave she too began to panic. Left on her own with the two children and her employer in such a state, the others not having returned, *"in fear for her own safety"* she took the baby and fled before she could be stopped by his mother. Mr Allison, who she passed on her way to the deck, took no apparent notice of them, and without stopping she reached the lifeboats. The baby was given to a steward as she climbed into boat 11. The steward, still holding the baby, followed her.

The families of Mr and Mrs Allison, we are told, viewed the actions of the nurse in a very unfavourable light. It seems, if it weren't for not knowing where her baby was, Mrs Allison would have left the ship. They held the nurse in someway responsible for the deaths of the Allisons. Bess's mother believing by rights it should have been her son-in-law, not the steward, who entered the lifeboat with her grandson.

Once aboard the *Carpathia* we are treated to another insight into Nurse Cleaver's character. Reunited with the other survivors of the Allison party she allowed the steward to visit the baby on a daily basis. At the same time she ignored the child's cries for, and outstretched arms to Mrs Allison's maid, Sarah Daniels, and persistently prevented her from getting anywhere near him. Seemingly, the nurse now had every intention of turning her role as the child's saviour to her own advantage. In the belief that control of the baby might not only offer her security, but also to profit in a more tangible way, she determined to retain her hold on him.

When the *Carpathia* docked at New York, Nurse Cleaver then encountered the waiting press. This presented a slightly different problem. In view of the loss of the rest of the family interest in the baby was intense, and it was vital that her true identity should not be revealed, further deception was necessary. She would not supply her surname, merely telling them her name was *"Jane"*. Here we learn that on the list of survivors the child and nurse were followed by a *"Miss K.T. Andrews"*, and therefore the reporters took it for granted this was who she must be ! Her story remained unquestioned, her identity unknown. One more difficulty arose for the newspapers, Nurse Cleaver's unattractive appearance did not quite match the supposed image their readers would have of how a heroine should look. Most took the obvious option and simply retouched the photograph before printing.

We are then taken forward in time many years to an event which at first might seem to have little to do with the nurse from the *Titanic*.

In 1929 Trevor Allison, a young man of 18, had died. As a baby he had been saved from the *Titanic* by his nurse. Neither his parents or his older sister Lorraine had survived. We are informed that his death was from ptomaine poisoning and following this the Allison estate passed to his guardians, his uncle and aunt.

In 1940 a young woman entered the public arena presenting herself as Trevor's sister, Lorraine, and therefore heir to the Allison estate. The aunt, by now a widow, stood to lose if this were proved to be true. The claims of Lorraine (now Lorraine Kramer), whose story apparently became *"even more farfetched"* when she employed a lawyer to look into her case, included her rescue from the *Titanic* by a Mr Hyde, whose true identity was then revealed as Thomas Andrews, a director of Harland and Wolff.

The identity of a *"Mrs. Gray"* who visited them as Andrews' sister is, however, in no such doubt. Nurse Cleaver had re-entered the story and was assisting Lorraine Kramer in her claims. How do we know this ? Well she was again using the name *"Mrs. Gray"* as she had back in 1909.

Lorraine Kramer's claims continued for a decade ending with her lawyer's death, and loss of his records in a fire. She finally moved west and out of the Allisons' lives.

Nurse Cleaver's role, it seems, had been to provide Lorraine Kramer with the ammunition for being able to make such a claim - it was she who had spanned the gap of nearly thirty years, and supplied Lorraine with family memories harking back to the *Titanic* and beyond.

I can't claim to have captured the whole intensity of the actions and character of Nurse Cleaver as depicted by Mr Lynch. Being her daughter has, in this instance, proved a great disadvantage. Try as I might I find it impossible to write of her in such a way as would truly re-create the essence of the woman he describes, and whose innermost thoughts are apparently known to him. It will, however, at least act as a reminder of what has been said to those who are aware of this story and a rough guide, I feel, to the decreasing few who are not.

Nevertheless his portrayal of my mother, which I have endeavoured to record as fairly as possible, is a picture I, and the rest of her family, did not recognise and could not believe in.

3

In Search of the Truth

The shock of learning what had been written about my mother seemed to overwhelm us completely but it was not a case of waiting for the initial shock to subside. Knowledge gradually gained that this story was not confined to a book but had from there formed a subplot for a television mini-series, *The Titanic,* and was also spread all over the internet, only added to the horror.

One thing was immediately apparent, something had to be done, it was out of the question that these appalling insults to my mother's memory should be allowed to stand. But where was I to start in the search for the truth, and the clearing of my mother's name ? Did this story have any foundation in reality whatsoever ?

As the family discussed the situation we realised there were several obvious routes that could be taken but it rather depended on how you viewed the information, which had been presented as factual. If indeed there had been such a murder case it would certainly have appeared in the newspapers, but not necessarily in the national press. In 1909, with far fewer options available to a young unmarried woman, crimes such as infanticide must have been very much more prevalent than they are today. Would all have made the mainstream press or were most only likely to have been reported at a local level ?

If the latter were true then we could expend a great deal of time searching through local newspapers, of which there were many, with perhaps little success. Compounded with the fact that we did not really know if there had ever been such a case we could find ourselves vainly seeking something that did not exist.

Surely it would be far more satisfactory to take a course of action that would prove conclusive one way or the other - namely, search for records of a trial. An exact date of 21st January 1909 had been quoted as when the baby's body was discovered, and it sounded as though a trial must have taken place relatively soon afterwards. This exercise would have the added advantage of picking up any cases that took place around that time, if for instance the story had been suggested by a real case, regardless of the defendant's name.

A few basic checks quickly confirmed that London and the surrounding area was covered by the Central Criminal Court, the rest of England, with certain exceptions, being divided into assize circuits. Therefore the records of the Central Criminal Court, more widely known as the Old Bailey would need to be consulted. These are preserved in the National Archives at the Public Record Office, Kew.

I approached the PRO with some trepidation. It is not in most people's experience to have to investigate the assertion that their mother was a child murderer. The family had all put forward their theories on what I should be looking for, and what I might expect to find. Having ordered a number of volumes, such as the Court Books and Calendar of Indictments, each of which covers a span of 3-6 years, I looked up more document references whilst waiting for these to come, so as to be ready to order again as soon as I was notified that my first batch had arrived. There in the class lists covering the Central Criminal Court, against the entries for the Depositions (CRIM 1/112) and also the Pardons (CRIM 1/583), both 1909, was the name that none of us really expected to see -

Alice Cleaver

Previously I had felt convinced that an imaginary account had just been plucked out of the air, to make a good story for the book. Others, by the date and background detailed, believed there might have been an actual case, but relating to someone of a different name.

However, as I began to view the documents there was no denying the fact that Alice Cleaver had been tried in March 1909, and found guilty of murdering her child in the January. Although surprised and taken aback on seeing the name, what I read only served to strengthen my belief that my mother did not commit this crime.

Throughout the day as I studied the various documents I learnt more and more about the case, consulting the actual witness depositions, record of her indictment, entry in the calendar of prisoners, her pardon and many other documents, including Home Office out letters. What seemed a terrible crime to be accused of was nothing compared to the heartbreaking story of poverty, ill health, desertion and desperation that unfolded.

From the many references to this case amongst the vast archives of the Public Record Office, plus more general sources, emerges the story of Alice Cleaver as related in the next chapter.

Returning briefly to the subject of the newspapers. Yes, this case was well reported both locally, and as it turned out nationally, no doubt due to the impact it had upon the public conscience. The salient facts that would lead one to the discovery of the truth appear there as well, but only to those who correctly study them. The real importance of the newspapers to this story will be revealed at a later stage.

4

The Story of Alice Cleaver

St Luke's Workhouse was situated in the pleasantly named Shepherdess Walk, just off the City Road, London, on the boundary of Shoreditch and Finsbury, an area well known to Charles Dickens. Indeed Edward Street, to the north of the workhouse, was renamed in honour of one of his most memorable characters, Mr Wilkins Micawber, from the 1850 novel *David Copperfield*, believed by some to be semi-autobiographical.

Micawber is perhaps best known for his philosophy on happiness and misery in relation to living within ones means. In the book fleeting reference is made to St Luke's itself when Mr Micawber first takes David Copperfield to his house in Windsor Terrace, also off the City Road. His servant, Clickett, informing young Mr Copperfield *"that she was 'a Orfling,' and came from St Luke's workhouse, in the neighbourhood"*. On one occasion he describes taking some of Mr Micawber's books for sale, and how that part of the City Road consisted mainly of bookstalls and bird-shops.

By dint of his connection with Mr Micawber, David Copperfield was also a frequent visitor to the pawnbroker's shop. Debt and the debtor's prison featured large in the lives of many of the mostly poor population occupying the area, as recalled in the

INFIRM WARDS & ADMINISTRATIVE OFF

H SAXON SN

OF ST LUKES WORKHOUSE. LONDON.

RITECT

Price 10s.

Scale Five Feet to One Statute Mile or 88 Feet to One Inch

19th-century rhyme and country dance - *Pop Goes the Weasel* - containing Cockney rhyming slang for pawn (pop) and tailor's iron (weasel):-

Up and down the City Road,
In and out the Eagle,
That's the way the money goes -
Pop goes the weasel !

The site of the *Eagle Tavern* (c.1825), opposite the workhouse, was originally a tea garden. The premises were put to a variety of subsequent uses including that of a music hall and the Grecian Theatre before demolition and rebuilding in 1901 as a public house.

The workhouse in Shepherdess Walk had been built in 1782, but by the 1860's improvements were sorely needed due to the then conditions. Henry Saxon Snell, Architect for the Holborn Union Poor Law Guardians, presented a series of plans for redevelopment. Building commenced in 1871 at the north end of the site, working southwards in sections. This in order to avoid problems that would have arisen, in housing all the inmates, had demolition and rebuilding been undertaken in one go.

The Architect noted how the somewhat unconventional plan of wards *"to be used as a combined dormitory and day room"*, was a feature of Mr Snell's already much admired work. Recognising that the inmates, on the whole, were not bedridden, this design allowed room for walking and provided seating at the large bay windows. According to *The Architect* the total cost of the building, to accommodate 930, was put at £36,000, this included fixtures and professional fees. Other reports suggest a total intake of 1,500 inmates. Improvements continued for some years with the building of the western section.

Even so, conditions remained austere, rules and regulations harsh, and the system itself much criticised - the workhouse was still dreaded.

Ordnance Survey Map, 1871 (left)
(Courtesy of Islington Local History Collections)
St Luke's Workhouse part way through construction

On arrival in the City Road the young Emily Cleaver turned into Shepherdess Walk and passing the famous *Eagle*, where just a few years earlier Marie Lloyd had made her debut, she applied at St Luke's Workhouse. At the time of admittance, by the master, she indicated that by calling she was a domestic servant from Warren Street, Islington. As someone who was both young and employed, her reason for entering the workhouse would only be revealed to the outside world nineteen days later when, after supper, Emily discharged herself from the care of the parish guardians and left St Luke's. In her arms she carried her infant daughter, Alice, just seventeen days old. The name of Alice's father remained Emily's closely guarded secret.

The story moves on as we leave the mother behind. Emily was to have little impact on her daughter's life until force of circumstance brought them together again.

~~~~~

In August 1908, Maria Davies became aware of and questioned her daughter Alice about her *"condition"*. They spoke of someone from Upper Holloway she had been keeping company with, and he was summoned to their rooms in Gladesmore Road, Tottenham, that evening, 12th August. It was on this occasion Alice was to learn for the first time that her young man was in fact married. Therefore, any expectation Mrs Davies might have had of bringing about a satisfactory conclusion to her daughter's situation, by arranging a speedy marriage, was quickly dispelled. This was to be the last time Alice would see the father of the child she was expecting.

When Alice Davies reached the age of sixteen, Maria Davies had had the task of breaking it to her that she, the child she had brought up as her own, was not in fact her daughter. Mrs Davies, now a widow and working as a laundress, had cared for Alice since she was three and a half years old, treating her as her daughter, training her to work alongside her as a laundress, and guiding her through her difficulties.

Shepherdess Walk as it is today

The Eagle and Shepherdess Cafe tangible reminders of the area's history (right) and plaque on The Eagle (below right)

St Luke's Workhouse, as with many such institutions gradually evolved from its former use into a hospital - St Matthew's Coming under the newly formed National Health Service in 1948 St Matthew's was closed in 1986 The main building being demolished thereafter

The surviving section now towered over by the modern offices that have replaced the grandeur of Saxon Snell's design (below left)

By the age of eight Alice had developed epilepsy, suffering fits lasting from a few minutes to half an hour, varying in frequency but at times recurring on a daily basis. Today these fits would probably be described as some sort of tonic-clonic seizure, previously known as a *grand mal*, in the majority of cases they would now be controllable by medication. There is some comfort in the knowledge that she would not have been aware of exactly what was happening to her, although she seemed to sense when they were about to occur, and no doubt felt sad and disorientated for a while afterwards, as well as being left with headaches and muscular pain.

On being told of her natural mother, Alice decided to revert to her original name and once again became Alice Cleaver, perhaps starting the chain of events which led to her being in a similar situation to her mother, Emily - pregnant and unmarried. In July 1908 Alice visited her mother at Inkerman Terrace, Kensington. A few years after her daughter's birth Emily had married a coachman and was by now in a fairly comfortable position. It was the first time mother and daughter had met since Alice was a young child.

In August, Alice's pregnancy was discovered, and her foster-mother, Mrs Davies, was directed by the relieving officer at Edmonton Infirmary to take her to Miss Manning, the superintendent of Edmonton Rescue Home for Girls. Miss Manning promised to assist with the confinement and arranged for her to enter St Mary's Home, Wellington Square, Chelsea, on 19th September. Presumably she was to stay there until the birth of her child at which time she would go to Edmonton Infirmary. Yet, only a week later, on the 25th, Alice was sent back to Gladesmore Road, following two fits which upset the others at the home. The former matron later explained in her deposition, that she would never have been accepted in the first place if they had been aware she was prone to these. Mrs Davies had described to the police the outward symptoms of Alice's condition - her eyes would roll, mouth foam and hands and feet become contorted. It must have been witnessing this that proved so distressing. Discrimination due to her epilepsy was just one more cross Alice Cleaver had to bear.

Inkerman Terrace, Kensington (above)

Wellington Square, Chelsea (below)

On 30th September, Alice entered Edmonton Workhouse. It seemed there was nothing she could do to escape her allotted fate, having herself been born in such an institution she was now faced with the prospect of staying in another one until her own child was born.

On 7th November, in the infirmary attached to the workhouse, Alice gave birth to a baby boy. She named him Reginald William Cleaver, and they both remained there for the next three weeks.

Towards the end of November, Alice left the workhouse infirmary returning to Gladesmore Road, with her baby. Mrs Davies was at that time away working in Kensington, but the landlady, Mrs Platt, wrote to let her know that they had turned up at Tottenham. Maria Davies went to see her foster-daughter, explaining that she would be unable to support her. Alice was obviously extremely upset and this resulted in a severe fit, brought on by the suggestion that she would have to spend the winter in the workhouse. Rather than do this she stayed with friends, apparently at the same address. Certainly this is where food was delivered to her on several occasions, sent by Miss Manning of Edmonton Rescue Home.

At 2 o'clock on the afternoon of Wednesday,16th December, Alice was taken by a lady visitor, who came from Edmonton Infirmary, to her mother Emily's home at Kensington. She had already expressed to Miss Manning her plans for obtaining work and living with Emily. But when she arrived at her mother's she had not yet made any arrangements for her baby.

Emily's husband didn't even know that Alice was his wife's child, born some years prior to their marriage, and whilst Emily may have been prepared to accommodate her daughter, perhaps without too much difficulty as they kept boarding rooms, the baby was another matter. It might have proved awkward to explain the presence there of an obviously unmarried woman with a young child, in what was presumably a respectable establishment. She therefore could not agree to Alice's pleas and refused to take both of them.

Alice left Kensington at 5pm with her son, unable to give any idea of her intentions, her mother assuming she would be entering the workhouse. She had, however, been advised of an institution, *The Haven for Homeless Little Ones*, Railway Approach, London Bridge, where he could be cared for on payment of a weekly fee. The information seems to have originated from someone who visited her at Gladesmore Road, with a view to placing the baby in a Dr Barnardo's home. When this proved unsuccessful *The Haven* was suggested instead, and by now Alice had obviously decided to try there.

By the time she reached London Bridge and *The Haven* it was after 6pm, and she was told at the door that it was probably too late to have her baby admitted that night. Upstairs she spoke to Mrs Wallis, the foundress, who noted the baby's details but confirmed that the matter could not be dealt with that night, she would have to come back on Friday.

On leaving, Alice met the lady who had answered the door to her. She entered into conversation, asking Alice how she had got on and if she had far to travel. As they walked across London Bridge, and in the direction of the Monument Railway Station, she informed Alice of her association with a Catholic home, in the Kilburn Park Road, asking whether she would be interested in placing her baby there. Again all the baby's details were noted, and a fee (presumably weekly) of five shillings was stated.

Until the baby could be accepted, on 20th January, Alice would have to stay in Kensington Workhouse and was instructed not to let the people there know about the Catholic home, but to say instead that a relative of her mother's was to take the baby. They arranged to meet on the 20th at Charing Cross, where the young mother was to part with baby Reginald, his birth certificate and the five shillings. She would be allowed to visit him at a later date, but when older he would be sent to Canada.

Bidding farewell at Kings Cross, Alice made her way along the Euston Road. A short time later becoming unwell she entered a confectioner's, and having passed her child to the shopkeeper, promptly fainted. She was taken by a policeman to the University College Hospital in Gower Street. After treatment, by a somewhat

Contrasting Scenes -

Railway Approach, London Bridge (above)
Southwark Annual, 1897
(Courtesy of Southwark Local Studies Library)

Charing Cross (right)
Ninety years after the alleged meeting with Mrs Gray

Apart from complete replacement of horses in favour of motorised
transport the view of Charing Cross has changed little since 1909

The actual cross erected in 1863 was modelled on the original 13th
century cross - the last in a chain of twelve marking the route of
Queen Eleanor's funeral cortege to Westminster Abbey in 1290

The original piers and railings fronting architect E M Barry's
Charing Cross Hotel were removed in 1958
The replicas built in 1989 were set further back
as a concession to modern traffic

sceptical doctor who diagnosed hysteria, Pc Hill accompanied her to Gower Street Railway Station and she completed her journey back to Kensington.

It was shortly before midnight when she arrived at the workhouse - Alice had travelled around London for nearly seven hours and was now refused entry. Continuing on to Inkerman Terrace, her mother had little choice but to allow her and the baby to stay for the night.

The following day, 17th December, Emily took her daughter and grandson to the workhouse infirmary. She was to visit them once during their stay, and to see her grandson for a final time on 20th January 1909.

At 9am that morning Alice called at Inkerman Terrace having left Kensington Workhouse on her way, as she told her mother and foster-mother, to the Catholic home at Kilburn. Emily gave her the five shillings she had written to ask for, and Alice left at about 11am. As her mother subsequently recalled in her deposition, her daughter was dressed in a brown jacket, blue skirt and wore a brown hat, the baby was wrapped in a shawl.

From here onwards doubt would later be cast on Alice Cleaver's movements, just as it would be on her description of what had occurred at *The Haven* - but this is *her* story so we will continue to follow her account for the time being.

By 11.30am Alice reached Charing Cross, ready for her pre-arranged meeting with the woman she had originally encountered back in December at *The Haven* - Mrs Gray. She would remember her as a tall woman of about thirty, aptly dressed in grey with auburn hair showing beneath a beaver hat. After some discussion of the terms previously put to her, she handed over the five shillings and Reginald's birth certificate, parting with her son.

Alice was to be contacted in a fortnight - but she never heard from Mrs Gray again !

By the early afternoon she was back home at Gladesmore Road, where she related to the landlady, Mrs Platt, what had taken place. On the following day (21st), when she saw her mother and

Stone Hall, Marloes Road, Kensington (above)
All that remains of the workhouse (later St Mary Abbots Hospital)
Seen through the arch of the modern housing development
that now surrounds it - Stone Hall was designed in the
the Jacobean style by Thomas Allom and dates from the 1840's

A relic from the former workhouse -
disused fountain (left)
adjacent to the Porter's Lodge
and (below) the inscribed verse

LORD.FROM.THY.BLESSED.THRONE.
THE.GRIEFS.OF.EARTH.LOOK.UPON.
GOD.BLESS.THE.POOR.
TEACH.THEM.TRUE.LIBERTY.
MAKE.THEM.FROM.STRONG.DRINK.FREE.
LET.THEIR.HOMES.HAPPY.BE.
GOD.BLESS.THE.POOR!

foster-mother in Kensington, she confirmed her baby had gone to the Kilburn home, but asked her mother to back her up if anyone should enquire by telling them the baby was in fact with a relative. A few days later she visited Miss Manning, of Edmonton Rescue Home, advising her, in accordance with the instructions from Mrs Gray, that the baby was being cared for by her mother's relations.

~~~~~

At 6.45 on the morning of 21st January 1909, William Sketcher, a platelayer working on the North London Railway between Broad Street, Haggerston and Dalston, had found the body of a baby. Dalston Police Station was informed and an officer went to the scene. When examined by a Surgeon at 8am the baby boy, weighing less than 8lbs and thought to be approximately three months old, was found to bear injuries consistent with having been thrown from a train, but had survived for an hour or two, finally succumbing to exposure. The baby, taken to the mortuary by Pc Snelgrove, was later buried unidentified.

On 31st January the police called at Mrs Davies' rooms at Gladesmore Road, and Inspector Divall questioned Alice on the whereabouts of her child. She then made a statement at Hackney Police Station, detailing events from the previous August, when her pregnancy was discovered.

From there the machinery of the law quickly swung into action. The next day (1st February), she was received into custody, the following week charged on remand with the wilful murder of her child - the baby's body being exhumed for identification purposes by order of the Home Secretary. On 24th February she appeared before magistrates at the North London Police Court and was committed for trial at the Old Bailey.

The account as given by Alice to the police, of events on that all-important day (20th January 1909), calling also upon statements made by her mother and foster-mother, has previously been related. Between leaving Kensington on the morning of the 20th, and them seeing her again on the 21st, she had described meeting Mrs Gray and then returning to Tottenham, but other witnesses threw some doubt on this.

It seems she did not in fact go to Gladesmore Road, on 20th January, after seeing Mrs Gray. According to Mrs Platt, Alice didn't arrive there until the 21st when she then mentioned having visited Mrs Lavender (a relative of her foster-mother's) the day before. Mrs Lavender herself corroborated this, referring to how Alice had unexpectedly turned up at her home in Upper Holloway, to all appearances having suffered a fit and being in need of food. Although 11 o'clock at night she claimed to be on her way from Kensington to Tottenham, and only stayed a very short time, leaving with some sandwiches when she realised Mrs Lavender was unable to put her up. Her baby, of whom Mrs Lavender was completely unaware, was not with her.

This left an unexplained gap in Alice's whereabouts for most of that day. Together with various witnesses who disputed her account concerning *The Haven* and the Kilburn home, plus one identification of her, this presented a pretty damning, if purely circumstantial case.

As far as *The Haven* was concerned, in their original depositions Jessie Gray (the clerk), Caroline Hames (the secretary) and Mrs Wallis (the foundress) could not recall having seen Alice. Admissions to *The Haven* were made between 9.30am and 5pm, she did not appear in their records and they had not taken her child. Jessie Gray denied having met her at Charing Cross.

The Police identified three children's homes in the Kilburn Park Road area. *The Orphanage of Mercy* at Randolph Gardens, was Church of England, not Catholic. Sister Rose confirmed they had two foster mothers by the name of Mrs Gray who took in children, but neither fitted the description, had authority to take the child or had done so. The identity of the one child admitted on 20th January was verified as being the five-month-old son of a widower, whose address was known. Both Mrs Grays denied being in London, meeting Alice and having taken any other child than those received via *The Orphanage of Mercy* in the previous year.

Central Criminal Court
Old Bailey

The location of many
famous trials -
built on the site of
Newgate Prison where
crowds once flocked to
see the public executions
held there until 1868
The cells can still be
viewed from beneath
the Viaduct Tavern

Alice seems to have had a piece of paper, which she said was given to her by Mrs Gray, referring also to St Augustine's Church, but again this was not Catholic and had no orphanage attached to it.

St Peter's Sisterhood, an Anglican community in St Augustine's parish, did not receive Alice's baby although they did admit older children. There was a Catholic orphanage (Miss Boyd's) in Percy Road, Kilburn, but they had not received any children for nearly three years, and as with the previous institution knew of no Mrs Gray.

Together with her identification by a railway porter (that placed her as the woman, with a baby, he had assisted at Broad Street, en route for Dalston), the final blow to her case was the clothing in which the baby's body was found, recognised by witnesses as being similar, indeed believed to be that worn by Alice's child.

~~~~~

On 8th March 1909, Alice Cleaver appeared in front of Mr Justice Phillimore at the Old Bailey, charged with the wilful murder of her son, Reginald William Cleaver. Over the course of the two-day trial, held in the Old Court, the all-male jury heard the *"Painful Life Story of a Child Mother"*, as the *Daily Sketch* put it. The over-riding sentiment of those present appears to have been one of a great deal of sympathy towards the defendant.

Judge Walter G F Phillimore would later become a Court of Appeal judge, be raised to the peerage, and ultimately take part in drafting the constitution of the Court of International Justice at The Hague.

In court Alice was represented by Mr Burnie and Mr Horace Samuel, having been granted legal aid under the Poor Prisoners Defence Act. The prosecution was undertaken by Mr Muir and Mr Graham Campbell. Approximately two dozen witnesses were called.

The interest of the newspapers seems to have been fired by two aspects of the trial. Under examination Alice, in the words of the *Daily Sketch* - *"maintained a wonderfully cool and collected demeanour, and told a most connected story"*. She did not display the normal emotions of those undergoing cross-examination at the Old Bailey, and perhaps did not fully appreciate what was going on.

The trial was adjourned at 5 o'clock in the afternoon, the jurors being sent to a hotel until resumption at 10.30 the following morning. On conclusion of the evidence the jury conducted a short deliberation returning after twenty minutes to deliver a verdict of *"Guilty"*, but at the same time very strongly recommending her to mercy.

Assuming the black cap, Mr Justice Phillimore passed the death sentence on Alice Cleaver, now a convicted murderer, and made the usual pronouncement that she would be hanged from the neck until dead, her body to be buried within the grounds of the prison in which she was to be confined at the time of execution - HMP Holloway !

Only then, on passing of the sentence, did Alice break down in tears, exclaiming *"I hope they will have mercy and help me."*

Although the judge had assured the court he would forward the jury's recommendation, her next few days were spent anxiously waiting in Holloway to learn whether the Home Secretary would indeed advise His Majesty King Edward VII to grant a reprieve.

The case seemed to have caught the public imagination and sympathy, letters appeared in the press questioning the passing of the death sentence prior to consideration by the King's advisors, where the judge and jury had so strongly recommended mercy.

The reprieve, when it came, was reported in the press a few days prior to 17th March 1909, on which date a formal *"Conditional Pardon"* was issued -

Conditional that is
on being kept in penal servitude for life !

A letter of the same date from the Home Office to Mr Justice Phillimore, notes the governor of Holloway Prison, Dr Scott, as commenting that *"having regard to the frequency and severity of the fits it is possible and even probable that she may deteriorate mentally and ultimately become certifiably insane"* - whatever the outcome she faced lifelong incarceration.

At this point I must break away from relating Alice Cleaver's story. To have been on the *Titanic* her release must have taken place before 10th April 1912. This to me was the glaring flaw in Mr Lynch's story. The weak link in the chain that might not bear scrutiny. So it was vital to discover exactly what had happened following her conviction and pardon.

Evidence of a file for her was discovered amongst the Home Office Registered Papers, but it was most disappointing to be told that it must have been destroyed.

The stress of trying to achieve my objective of proving my mother's innocence, whilst at the same time still suffering from shock over the allegations made, led to what later appeared to be a quite straightforward process becoming much more complicated than was in fact necessary.

H M Prison Holloway

*Built in 1852 (based in part on Caesar's Tower at Warwick Castle)
It was demolished in the 1970's and replaced with a featureless
red brick structure - the exterior of which gives no indication of
its predecessor's history as the City House of Correction
For most of this century it has been used solely for the detention
of female prisoners - the suffragettes including Mrs Pankhurst
numbered among its more famous residents*

5

To London and Back

Whilst we felt the information we were looking for was still to be found at PRO Kew, a stumbling block, albeit hopefully only a temporary one, seemed to have been reached. The archives are so vast that there was a temptation to spend day after day there. However, on balance it appeared it might prove more rewarding to change the direction of the research away from Alice Cleaver's prison life and concentrate on trying to establish what had eventually happened to her.

Where and when did she die ? After all, regardless of what records existed concerning her imprisonment one thing she must have had was a death certificate. Although an option previously considered, only now did the rather open-ended search it might entail seem worthy of pursuit. All who have spent a morning in central London heaving the quarterly death indexes off the shelves and avoiding the elbows of the other searchers, will understand my reluctance to do this for no good reason. In theory, judging by her age, she could have lived for another fifty years or more after entering prison, so I had to be prepared to cover upwards of 200 volumes.

Nevertheless, as the research at Kew had progressed, I felt I had come to know enough about the severity of her health condition to believe she was unlikely to have survived for very many years. In the early part of the century epilepsy, like many other disorders, could not be controlled as well as it is nowadays.

It was mid to late morning when, armed with prepared pages divided into years and quarters, I entered the search rooms and commenced my task. Fortunately, not only were there comparatively few people about but there was little demand for the group of years in which I was interested. As I advanced from year to year, moving along the rows of volumes and occasionally switching positions with other searchers, I was able to work quite quickly.

Having decided to start from the beginning of 1909, the first three years were covered without a single Alice Cleaver being located. A brief break in the monotony occurred in the first quarter of 1912 with the discovery of an Alice M. Cleaver who died in the district of Marylebone, London, it was sad to see her age given as *"0"*. Continuing on, the next entry appeared precisely three years later, this was also in a London district - Wandsworth. Again another young death, although at least she had reached the age of 26. Remembering Alice Cleaver's age at the time of her trial this entry seemed a possibility, but what would she have been doing south of the river in Wandsworth ? In the last quarter of that same year another Alice Cleaver also from a London district was found. She, however, could be immediately ruled out as being in a different age group.

I continued the search for a few more years but kept thinking back to the 1915 entry. It was difficult to know quite what to do, it wasn't as if there were a specified number of years to search. How far should I persist in looking through the death indexes when this might prove to be the one I was after ? To search further would then be a waste of time and energy. There was no question of obtaining the certificate that day; should I order it and return home only to find it was a red herring, which would then necessitate another visit to continue my search ?

Eager to get on, short of going to the Wandsworth District Registrar and back, was there any other path I could take to discover more about a possible Wandsworth connection ? It was certainly not unreasonable to suppose she could have been transferred from Holloway, north London, the first place of her imprisonment, to Wandsworth. Not only because of the existence of the prison there, but also the various other institutions in the area. But was that just wishful thinking ?

Knowing the Metropolitan Archives to be only a few minutes walk away, they seemed well worth a visit. It was probable that records of at least some of these institutions might be deposited there, and I had a feeling that those for Wandsworth Prison could be amongst them. This proved correct, but unsuccessful. It was immediately apparent from studying the list of holdings that prisoners' records of the date only covered males, and I found patients' admission registers of the various mental institutions heavily restricted for that period. I later confirmed that women were no longer detained at Wandsworth Prison in the 1900's. Somewhat frustrated I brewed the matter over during a lunch break, deciding the most logical thing to do would be to go back to my search of the death indexes; continue for a set number of years, review my results at the end of these, leaving enough time to order any certificates.

During the afternoon I worked my way through another thirty years of the indexes, compiling a short list of half a dozen possibles, yet none seemed as likely as the one first found. I would, I suppose, have to be patient, order the 1915 death certificate and await its arrival to see what it could tell me. Only, the thought of waiting five days seemed then like waiting an eternity. Impatience got the better of me, and one of the family agreed to obtain the certificate direct from the district registrar.

From this I learnt that Alice Cleaver of Aylesbury, a domestic servant, had died on 12th February in the *Hostel of God* at Clapham Common. Certain details tied in, i.e. obviously her age with that given at the trial, and also a remark about her father's name not being known. There was no indication of any connection with prison life, although I can't exactly explain how I expected this to be shown. The reference to Aylesbury seemed superfluous, yet mysterious. If she *was* from there, how strange that her death took place in London.

CERTIFIED COPY of an **ENTRY OF DEATH**

Pursuant to the Births and **Deaths Registration Act 1953**

HC514315

D. Cert.
S.R.

Registration District **WANDSWORTH**

1915. Death in the Sub-district of **Clapham** in the **County of London**

No.	When and where died	Name and surname	Sex	Age	Occupation	Cause of death	Signature, description, and residence of informant	When registered	Signature of registrar
Columns:—	1	2	3	4	5	6	7	8	9
394	Twelfth February 1915 Hostel of God 29 North Side	Alice CLEAVER	Female	26 Years	of Aylesbury Domestic Servant. Spinster	(1) Phthisis pulmonalis Certified by M. Mackintosh M.D.	Ida Pinnott Lady Superintendent Hostel of God 29 North Side Clapham Common	Sixteenth February 1915	Ida Pinnott Registrar.
					name and occupation of father unknown.				

Certified to be a true copy of an entry in a register in my custody.

DMRure .... Superintendent Registrar.

.... 1st July 1998 .... Date.

On making further enquiries it was disappointing to find that the surviving *Hostel of God* records did not cover the period I was interested in. Although her burial was traced to Streatham Cemetery neither did this yield any more in the way of explanation.

I was none the wiser, had I found her or not ? Perhaps working on the basis that she could have died in 1915, but by no means taking this for granted, I would return to Kew, and in the absence of anything else, conduct a more thorough search of some of the Home Office correspondence.

Death Certificate (left)
By Kind Permission of the Office for National Statistics

Justice with her scales, Old Bailey (above)

The Public Record Office, Kew (below)

6

Let the Truth Speak for Itself

On a previous visit to the Public Record Office a foray into the Criminal Case Entry Books - Out Letters (HO 163) had uncovered the communication from the Home Office to Alice Cleaver's trial judge. This is where the thoughts of the governor of Holloway Prison, regarding her condition, had been recorded.

A straightforward search for her name in the alphabetical indexes contained within each volume (covering on average only some six weeks), over a reasonably lengthy span of time, had proved fruitless as regards establishing what had happened to her. The problem, as I had come to realise part way through the search, was that the alphabetical indexes were not necessarily comprehensive to the contents of the volume i.e. Cleaver might not appear under 'C' but there still might have been an out letter. I discovered this when I picked at random a couple of letters and then unsuccessfully sought to find the person they referred to in the relevant section of the alphabetical index. Also incorporated within every volume were a series of subject indexes, each of which required a search in its own right.

Now looking through again with a specific time frame in mind, I was able to concentrate my efforts and check each of these different sections and the whole of the alphabetical index thoroughly. Even so, just the period from the trial to the spring of 1915 involved some 35 volumes, and I wondered whether I was really on the right track when the first volume I searched, that covering February 1915, appeared bereft of entries for Alice Cleaver.

However, a break-through came rather more quickly than anticipated, I had found a letter concerning her and what is more it linked with the rather obscure reference on the 1915 death certificate. The Home Office letter, in reply to a petition from the prisoner, asked the governor to inform her that the Secretary of State *"finds no grounds to justify him in recommending compliance with the prayer thereof."* Alice Cleaver was at that date, 21st August 1911, in Aylesbury Prison.

Later in the day another break-through, when a chance conversation with one of the archivists led to the realisation that the file in the Home Office Registered Papers (HO 144), previously believed to have been destroyed, was in fact still in existence. From this the final missing chapter of Alice Cleaver's life can be revealed.

On obtaining her file the judge's notes contained therein provided a further insight to the proceedings at the Old Bailey.

The case as reviewed all these years later, can only be said, as was put forward by her defence counsel at the time, to rest on circumstantial evidence; albeit pretty strong. No one actually witnessed the child being thrown from a train. At the identity parade the railway porter picked Alice out of a line of some fourteen women, declaring her to be the woman, with a baby, he had spoken to and assisted at Broad Street Station, who had gone past her intended destination of Dalston. However, the fireman who also recalled the woman at the station, faced with the same line-up, failed to pick her out. By the time she arrived at Mrs Lavender's that night the child was definitely not with her. The woman in charge of the infants' nursery at Kensington Workhouse attested that *"she* [Alice] *was indifferent to the child".* Following investigation by the police, the young mother's explanation of her child's whereabouts, was simply not accepted by them, the judge or the jury.

The defence chipped away at prosecution evidence by getting the platelayer, who found the baby's body, to confirm that more than one line passed that location. Vaccination marks that were claimed as part of identification of the body were shown to be common, as was the baby's clothing. Either the latter had not been observed by the women questioned on this, or else they wavered, becoming rather less definite under cross-examination.

At the trial Alice's answers to the questioning provide a rather different story than that given in her original deposition. Obviously, as *The Times* had mentioned, when first reporting the case in February 1909, she made several conflicting statements to the police. She still maintained her innocence, insisting she had returned to Gladesmore Road, Tottenham on the afternoon of 20th January, after handing over baby Reginald at Charing Cross. But receiving no answer there, in the words of the *Daily Mail* *"she had wandered about London"* both on foot and using a variety of transport, from underground train and electric tram to the green car.

Her first destination was her mother's at Kensington, arriving sometime between 5 and 5.30 pm, again she saw no one, despite waiting around for a couple of hours. She vehemently denied obtaining a ticket to Dalston or being at Broad Street Station, as she was booked to travel via Kings Cross. She then decided to visit Mrs Lavender, walking all the way to Upper Holloway, which in view of her lameness took the best part of two and a half hours. Unfortunately Mrs Lavender was unable to accommodate her so she left, managing to find a room for the night in the locality, and returning the next day (21st) to Gladesmore Road as Mrs Platt stated.

The judge, Justice Phillimore, who seemed perhaps a man ahead of his time in the compassion he showed towards the defendant, was concerned that no affiliation summons had been taken out against the baby's father. This, the responsibility of the relieving officer (appointed by the Poor Law Guardians), should have enabled more tangible support to have been given to Alice. In answer to the judge's questions, Alice confirmed that she had written to the father for money but had received no reply.

Judge Phillimore thought there to be little doubt that she had carried out the murder, but also believed that she *had* visited *The Haven* in an effort to find proper accommodation for her child. Mrs Platt, the landlady, verified on cross-examination, not only someone calling from Dr Barnardo's home, as Alice had stated, but also that they left an address for *The Haven*.

The staff of this institution, in their original depositions, tended to throw doubt on having seen Alice, but under examination at the trial certain interesting facts were revealed. The secretary of *The Haven* admitted the defendant had given a good description of the room there. The foundress noted that she was expecting someone to call back. The clerk - Jessie Gray - said that someone had called in that week about a child.

In addition to her knowledge of *The Haven,* its interior and operating hours, she also seemed to have a degree of knowledge about the home in Kilburn. It has been suggested that *"no such woman* [Mrs Gray] *or institution could be found."* This is not entirely true. Certainly an orphanage in Randolph Gardens, just off Kilburn Park Road, did exist and *was* found. Sister Rose, from this institution, made a deposition and appeared at the trial.

The discrepancy with Alice Cleaver's story lay in the fact that it was a Church of England home, not Roman Catholic as she claimed to have been told by Mrs Gray. Believing for a moment that she had been told this, then Mrs Gray could have introduced the Catholic element as a reason for Alice not to mention the matter to the Church of England inclined people at Kensington Workhouse. Also, it has been shown that a number of women by the name of Gray were connected to the various institutions, but evidence of their existence should not be taken as evidence of their involvement.

It may be that Alice had been able to gain information from the other girls at Kensington Workhouse, to name one possible source, or else just hit upon coincidences. But if she really felt the need to contrive such a story, wouldn't she have been worried that it would fall apart once the police started looking into it ? Perhaps it was only supposed to be enough to quieten the questions of those closest to her, who would have no interest in delving too deeply if in doubt. Police involvement was probably the last thing she expected.

Alice's natural mother had shown some agreement to allowing her daughter to live with her, but could not take the child as well. Thwarted in attempts to find a place for her baby, without tying herself to many years of struggling to pay for his upkeep, no doubt she did feel desperate and unable to think clearly. Still only two and a half months after giving birth, and with her recurring epilepsy, she could not have envisaged any prospect of her life turning out as successfully as her mother's had after a similar incident.

It seems probable that, in the words of Justice Phillimore - *"The action was very deliberate and done to escape the restraint of the workhouse".*

But I have one lingering doubt, was she really aware of what she was doing ? Could she have suffered from post-epileptic automatism, under which it is now recognised people can un-knowingly act in a seemingly bizarre or even violent manner ? Mrs Lavender testified at the Old Bailey her belief that, on the day in question, Alice had suffered a fit. The reason the porter remem-bered and was able to identify her was that she had been confused, missed her station, and needed to be helped into a compartment.

If she was affected by post-epileptic automatism, on recovery she would have been completely unaware of her actions, or even how she had got from A to B. I wonder, could she perhaps have subconsciously begun to reconstruct the missing period with what she had originally intended to do.

In any event this is the sort of case which allows students of history to reflect on how greatly things have changed within a relatively short space of time. The Infanticide Act of 1922 meant that in effect this crime (killing of a child within its first year) was no longer punishable by death where the balance of the mother's mind was found to be disturbed and the capital sentence itself is of course now abolished. But most of all no counsel worth their salt would miss the opportunity, now available to them, of introducing post-epileptic automatism as a prime factor in her defence.

Aylesbury Prison, Buckinghamshire
(Courtesy of Richard J Johnson)

After the pardon came through Alice Cleaver was to spend only another three weeks in Holloway before being transferred away from London to Aylesbury Prison on 8th April 1909.

The detail of her day-to-day life in prison is not documented. Only her regular medical examinations every few months, determining the state of her epilepsy and more general health, appear. But in any case the real interest is in how her release came about, rather than what took place during her incarceration.

On 21st August 1911, as previously related, the out letters recorded a reply to what was clearly a petition for reduction of sentence, advising that her request could not be met.

Her next recorded petition was also to prove unsuccessful. It would not be long before she *was* released but this would arise only after the failure to find suitable long-term alternative accommodation, and the onset of further serious illness.

Early in January, following direct intervention by the Duchess of Bedford (Adeline, widow of the 10th Duke), Alice was released. This, however, was not January of 1912, 1913 or even 1914. She had not been released at such a premature date that - *"By April 1912, she was on board the Titanic"*.

Alice Cleaver, who in the space of her short life suffered far more than her fair share of misery, had for some time been dying from acute phthisis, a form of tuberculosis.

Her petition of February 1913, in which she requested to know how long her sentence might last, followed by a routine medical report indicating her health had not deteriorated, had been met by a Home Office reply on 13th March. This advised *"that her case shall be considered later but it is too soon to decide on any reduction of sentence."* At the same time, presumably unknown to Alice, her file records that the Mental Deficiency Act might be brought into use as the most appropriate way of handling her case, and it was noted for review in twelve months time.

The correspondence of 1914 details the enquiries that were being made to find a suitable institution to which she might be transferred. But on 21st October, before any solution could be found to the problem, the medical officer reported Alice Cleaver to be suffering from phthisis (acute consumption). The decision was taken to keep her at HMP Aylesbury, Dr Fox having stated *"she is receiving better care than would be possible were she released."*

However, by January of 1915 the Dowager Duchess of Bedford, noted for her good works, was taking a special interest in the case, having *"secured a place for her in the Hostel for the Dying, Clapham Common"*. As Alice drew closer to death the authorities, agreeing to the provisional arrangements put in hand, released her on licence so she might spend her last remaining days in the more comfortable, compassionate surroundings of a hospice.

This is how Alice Cleaver came to return to London on 19th January 1915, left any longer it would have been too late for her to be moved, and she would have died within the confines of the prison where she had been for almost six years. She was to survive her release from prison for just over three weeks, dying on 12th February at the *Hostel of God*.

In case you are still in any doubt - no, she was not my mother, she was not the nurse on the *Titanic*. For how could this young woman ever have escaped her mapped-out destiny. Her release to freedom, such as it was, at least allowed her to die peacefully as a free woman, rather than as a convict.

~~~~~

At peace she should have remained. Was it not enough for her life to have been destroyed because of the misuse and desertion of one man ? Had she not already faced the verdict of one jury and paid for her crime without now having a multitude of other crimes heaped on her shoulders at a time when she was either in prison or had long since died ? Thank God for her sake that the judge she met with in life was Judge Phillimore.

Trinity Hospice
Clapham Common

formerly

The
Hostel
of
God

Once home to Architect Sir Charles Barry (who died there in 1860)
now displaying a blue plaque in recognition - his son E M Barry
designed the Charing Cross Hotel pictured earlier

Its present use as a hospice was established at
the turn of the century by an Anglican Sisterhood
From The Hostel of God has grown the now secular
Trinity Hospice, justly proud of its history and quality of care

In some ways learning of her real mother and then meeting with her does not appear to have been an entirely good thing, it gave her the glimpse of a new life, but came too late.

Had she been of better health she could, like her own mother, have overcome the difficulties of unmarried mother-hood. But with her illness always to contend with she followed inexorably her path in life. When deterred from one course of action she did not have the wherewithal to persist in it.

Despite the discrimination of some, she met with kindness and compassion from many others. From her foster-mother Maria Davies; her natural mother who did not disown her on her reappearance and stated *"I . . . would have done what I could for her"*; Miss Manning at Edmonton Refuge who made considerable efforts on her behalf; the policeman who took her under his wing when she fell ill in the Euston Road and paid her fare home out of his own pocket; the judge, Justice Phillimore; the all-male jury and at the end of her life the Duchess of Bedford. Why then is compassion for her now lacking in what we consider a more enlightened, humane and non-discriminatory age ? Should this be taken as a scathing indictment on the hypocrisy of our society, or is it more a case of the vociferous minority letting their true feelings show ?

For those readers who are genuinely interested in the truth, or those sceptics who still might not take my word for this - Let the Truth Speak for Itself. On the following pages are reproduced documents substantiating pertinent facts of the case:-

1. *Pardon and penal servitude for life - March 1909*
   Central Criminal Court: Pardons 1909
   CRIM 1/583

2. *Might ultimately become certifiable - March 1909*
   Home Office: Criminal Case Entry Books: Out Letters
   HO 163/42

3. *Still in prison - February 1913*
   Home Office: Registered Papers - Supplementary - 1910
   HO 144/1034/176577

4. *Too soon to be released - March 1913*
   Home Office: Criminal Case Entry Books: Out Letters
   HO 163/67

5. *Institutional accommodation sought - August 1914*
   Home Office: Registered Papers - Supplementary - 1910
   HO 144/1034/176577

6. *Transfer from Prison to Hospice - January 1915*
   Home Office: Registered Papers - Supplementary - 1910
   HO 144/1034/176577

7. *Release on Licence - January 1915*
   Home Office: Registered Papers - Supplementary - 1910
   HO 144/1034/176577

Edward R & I.

Whereas Alice Cleaver was, at the Central Criminal Court, on 9th March, 1909, convicted of Murder and sentenced to Death,

We in consideration of some circumstances humbly represented unto Us, are Graciously pleased to extend Our Grace and Mercy unto the said Alice Cleaver and to grant unto her Our Pardon for the offence of which she so stands convicted, on Condition that she be kept in Penal Servitude for Life,

7/0577
Alice Cleaver

Conditional Pardon

Our

Our Will and Pleasure
therefore is that you do give the
necessary directions accordingly;
And for so doing this shall be
your Warrant.

Given at Our Court at St James's
the Seventeenth day of March
1909 in the ninth year of
Our reign

To Our Trusty and Well beloved
Our Justices for the Central
Criminal Court.
The High Sheriff for the County
of London
The Governor of Our Prison at
Holloway
and all others whom it may

concern

By His Majesty's Command.

Gladstone

the reports received from time to time as to her mental
and physical condition.

I have the honour to be,

My Lord,

Your Lordship's obedient Servant,

176,577.

17th March, 1909.

My Lord,

I have the honour, by direction of the Secretary
of State, to acquaint your Lordship that he has had under
his consideration all the circumstances in the case of
Alice Cleaver, convicted before you at the Central
Criminal Court of murder and sentenced to death, and that
he has felt justified in advising His Majesty to respite
the capital sentence with a view to its commutation to
penal servitude for life.

Dr. Scott, the Governor of Holloway Prison who
has had the prisoner under his observation both before
and since the trial reports that she is undoubtedly
epileptic and that in his opinion having regard to the
frequency and severity of the fits it is possible and
even probable that she may deteriorate mentally and
ultimately become certifiably insane. As your Lordship
is aware it is in accordance with the usual practice to
commute in the first instance to penal servitude for life;
but the question of how long and under what conditions
the prisoner will be detained is deferred for future
consideration and will in this case depend largely upon

the

The Honourable

Mr. Justice Phillimore,

&c.,   &c.,   &c.

PRISON ...
2 ... 1913

REDUCTION OF SENTENCE

HOME OFFICE
28 FEB. 1913
RECEIVED

176 577/23

PETITION 176577

Register Number.	Name in full.	Age on Conviction.	Conduct in Prison.
			*Here state "Good," "Bad," "Fair," or "Indifferent."
j 5	Alice Cleaver	20	Good

Conviction.		Offence.	Sentence.	Marks for remission forfeited or not earned through any cause except illness.	
Court and Place.	Date.			During last 12 months.	Previously.
C.C.C. London	2-3-09	Wilful murder	Death Commuted to P.S. for Life	2	8

P. W. Prison Aylesbury

26th February 1913

W. H. Winder
Governor.

PREVIOUS CONVICTIONS. (Those proved in court to be marked*)

The previous convictions will only be given in the *first* petition after each conviction. In subsequent petitions the number of previous convictions will be summarized and a reference made by date to the first petition.

Sentence.	Court and Place.	Date.	Offence.	Name.
		Nil		

The Petitioner must not write on this margin.

To the Right Honourable His Majesty's Principal Secretary of State for the Home Department.

THE PETITION OF THE ABOVE-NAMED PRISONER HUMBLY SHEWETH :—

Asks for a fixed sentence

That she wishes to bring before your Lordship her sad case, hoping that you will take it again into consideration together with the time she has now completed, and begs of your Lordship, if it be possible to give her a stated sentence however small the remission of the same might be, she would be very thankful.

Your Humble Petitioner
Alice Cleaver

No. 249

(9539)

No. 4

(HO 163/67)

175,577/23.

The Under Secretary of State requests that the
Governor of Aylesbury Prison will be so good as to
inform the convict Alice Cleaver (j. 5), in reply to
her petition of the 25th ultimo, that the Secretary
of State has decided that her case shall be considered
later but it is too soon to decide on any reduction
of sentence.

Whitehall,
        13th March, 1913.

THE BOARD OF CONTROL,

66, *Victoria Street, S.W.*

28th August, 1914.

- Sir,

re Alice Cleaver, Aylesbury Prison.
H.O.File 176577/25

I have the honour to inform you that the Board
of Control have been in correspondence with the Warden
of the Incorporation of National Institutions in regard
to the possibility of finding accommodation for the
above-named case in one of the Institutions managed by
the Incorporation. The Board have now received from the
Incorporation a letter, a copy of which is herewith
enclosed, in which it is stated that the Committees of
Stoke Park and Whittington Hall feel that cases of this
kind ought not to be admitted to either Institution.

I have the honour to be,

Sir,

Your obedient Servant,

S.P. Byrne

Chairman.

The Under Secretary of State,

Home Office.

TELEPHONE
GERRARD 4700

Jun. 13. 15

51, BERKELEY SQUARE,
W.

Dear Mr. Dryhurst,

May I draw y-
attention to the case of
Alice Cleaver, a convict
in Aylesbury Prison - She
was slightly mentally
deficient when she came
nearly 5 years ago,
sentenced for infanticide,
& has epileptic fits -
She is now very gentle,

& certainly more intelligent,
but has developed
phthisis, & Dr. Fox the
medical officer thinks
her lungs are giving way
rapidly - So much so, that
she recommends her being
sent to a Home for the—

Dying, should her release
be granted.

I have secured a place
for her in the Hostel for
the Dying, Clapham Common,
where she wd receive every
attention, & she can be
removed there when you
give consent. In the
usual

course her case would
come up for consideration
abt this time, but it
would be impossible
to place her in any of
her certified Homes.

Yours sincerely
Adeline M. Bedford

Jan. 13. 15
51, BERKELEY SQUARE,
W.

Dear Mr Dryhurst,

May I draw yr attention to the case of Alice Cleaver, a convict in Aylesbury Prison - She was slightly mentally deficient when she came nearly 5 years ago, sentenced for infanticide, & has epileptic fits - She is now very gentle, & certainly more intelligent, but has developed phtisis, & Dr Fox the medical officer thinks her lungs are giving way rapidly - So much so, that she recommends her being sent to a Home for the Dying, should her release be granted.

I have secured a place for her in the Hostel for the Dying, Clapham Common, where she wd receive every attention, & she can be removed there when you give consent. In the usual course her case would come up for consideration abt this time, but it would be impossible to place her in any of the certified Homes -

Yours vry sincry
Adeline M. Bedford

Letter from the Duchess of Bedford - HO 144/1034/176577 (left)
Transcript of same (above)

FOR P.R.O.

Subnumber _____ _____

Registration HO 144/1034

176577

27a

No. 7

(HO 144/1034/176577)

C

CONVICT.
NOTIFICATION OF RELEASE ON LICENCE.

General Register Number _J. 5_

Name in full _Alice Cleaver_

Date of Licence _16th January_ 19 15 .

H. O. Number on Licence _176577_
_9704_

Date of Release _19th January_ 19 15 .

Period for which Licence
is granted—as stated in } _Life_ Years, _"_ Days.

endorsement on Licence }

* Date on which above }

period will expire } * (treated as an appellant _Nil_ days)

W. H. Winder GOVERNOR.

H. M. Prison, _Aylesbury_

19th January 19 15 .

(The space below this line is for use in the Directors' and Commissioners' Office)

Submitted to the Secretary of State.

21. 1. 19 15 .

7

Summing Up - The Weight of Evidence

At the end of a trial it is customary for the judge to sum up and direct the jury. But it is not necessary to sum up in the usual sense of these words in the case of my mother, Nurse Cleaver. The jury would not be due to retire shortly to consider their verdict, they would already have been dismissed, as would the charge of murder. With the evidence presented in the last chapter even the most dogged of prosecutors must surely have conceded the case.

Despite all the miscarriages of justice that still occur in the civilized world, seldom has there been a greater injustice than that accorded to Nurse Cleaver. No longer alive to face her accusers, the trial held in her absence and without defence counsel being present. In pursuing the case so many years after it happened, the prosecution has dragged into the dock not the original defendant but someone completely unconnected with the proceedings.

~~~~~

Where this case differs from all others is that it is the guilty party who has a cast-iron alibi, not the innocent accused. One could almost envisage the following courtroom cross-examination taking place:-

Counsel:	'Do you deny that having served a sentence for murder you later gained work as a nurse and travelled on board the *Titanic* ? '
Alice:	'I do deny it sir, it is untrue.'
Counsel:	'Where then were you at around midnight on 14th/15th April 1912 ? '
Alice:	'Sir, I was in bed asleep.'
Counsel:	'Would you confirm to the court your place of abode at that time ? '
Alice:	'I was in Aylesbury Prison.'

~~~~~

The documents irrefutably show that the young woman who murdered her child had not been released by, or even during, April 1912. There was no question of her ever having been free to be on the *Titanic*. The weight of evidence balances not against Nurse Cleaver, but against her accuser.

How then could Mr Lynch in his book *(Titanic: An Illustrated History)* make the following statements ?

"Three years earlier she had murdered her own baby son. Although tried and convicted, she had been released on the grounds that her crime was an act of desperation following desertion by the child's father, to whom she was not married."

"On January 21, 1909, several platelayers working on the North London Railway made a grisly discovery - the tiny body of a baby boy, apparently thrown from a train the night before. Within weeks, Alice Mary Cleaver of Tottenham was arrested for the murder of her own child. Although she maintained that she had given the baby to a "Mrs. Gray" of an orphanage in Kilburn, no such woman or institution could be found. Alice was convicted of her crime but the jury recommended leniency and she eventually went free. By April 1912, she was on board the Titanic working as a nurse for the Hudson Allison family of Montreal."

After all it is these statements on which his whole case against my mother, Nurse Cleaver, her supposed murder of a child and her overall character, rests.

Has the author misled himself and therefore everyone else ?

In stating that *"she eventually went free"* and *"by April 1912, she was on board the Titanic"*, the reader could be forgiven for assuming him to be in possession of conclusive evidence to that effect. He does not state the actual date but the word *"eventually"* implies that he is aware of the timescale and perhaps he does not want to clutter his account with too many dates ? But there is no such information to show that *"she"* was free prior to the sailing of the *Titanic,* no such documentation, no such evidence whatsoever, for the one simple reason - she was not free. On the contrary, it was to be nearly three more years before she would be released, and that was only due to her impending death. Otherwise she was likely to have remained incarcerated until her childbearing years were over.

~~~~~

At the 1909 trial the guilty verdict was swiftly followed by the passing of the death sentence. Mr Lynch fails to mention in his book that her murder conviction resulted in this, the ultimate sentence. Had he stated she was to be hanged for her crime, would so many have accepted so readily the story of such a premature release ? Likewise had he mentioned her epilepsy and its severity, one might have begun to wonder how she could have hidden symptoms so obvious and recurrent from her employers.

Would someone who had a death sentence for infanticide passed on them at that date really have been allowed free to walk the streets and take up employment as a children's nursemaid only three years later ? Common sense would say this was extremely unlikely. This is to presume that her mother and foster-mother would have done nothing to prevent their daughter taking a highly responsible post, caring for young children, for which she was totally ill-equipped and wherein disastrous consequences might be foreseen. Also to presume that the police and probation service were derelict in their duty in allowing a convicted child murderer who would have been released on licence, to evade their supervision and jurisdiction.

Finally, that she herself, having escaped the noose and obtained her freedom, would risk all by breaking the law to present herself as a nursemaid. It may only have been a summary offence for a servant to gain employment by deception. However, it is debatable, when taking into account her record and the public safety, that any magistrate would have felt it prudent not to have strongly urged the revoking of her licence.

Even disregarding all these considerations - first it is necessary to believe, notwithstanding her notoriety, using the very name in which she had been convicted, she brazenly entered employment envisaging no problems in that most determined hotbed of gossip and inquisition - the servants' hall. Then, not long after, at the drop of a hat, far from her homeland, adopted false names to hide her identity ? Logic would have questioned why, unless willing to accept almost certain recognition, she didn't adopt a false name from the start.

But common sense or logic clearly does not come into it or I would not now need to be discussing a situation that never arose, events that never took place.

~~~~~

Only conclusive evidence of the facts could justify anyone, especially a historian, in stating *"she eventually went free. By April 1912, she was on board the Titanic working as a nurse for the Hudson Allison family of Montreal."*

In the light of this, let us try again to see what documentation is available to support the author's statements. What compelling evidence could have led him to the conclusions he reached. Well, in lieu of any information to the contrary from Mr Lynch I can only assume the answer is - none !

There is commentary and evidence aplenty on the trial and the events leading up to it, in both national and local newspapers of the day, as there is of the sentence handed down. Newspapers covering the case were unanimous in their reporting of the outcome - the defendant was sentenced to death for the murder of her child. It is true that the jury did ask for mercy because of her circumstances, but it must be stressed that this was mercy in order that her life be spared. At that date the death sentence was mandatory for those found guilty of murder, infanticide included.

"UTTER DESPAIR
Child-Mother Condemned to Death
JUDGE'S EMOTION
We find her guilty; but knowing that she was deserted and neglected by the child's father, and had been forced to utter distraction, we very strongly recommend her to mercy."
"With evident emotion the Judge (Justice Phillimore) yesterday passed the death sentence, but before doing so said that he would take every care that the recommendation for mercy was forwarded to the right quarters and he had no doubt it would meet with every attention from a most humane and careful Home Secretary."
(The Daily Sketch, Wednesday March 10th 1909)

"North London Child Murder
Death Sentence at Old Bailey"
"The jury found defendant guilty, but recommended her to mercy. Sentence of death was passed."
(Islington Daily Gazette, Wednesday March 10th 1909)

When the reprieve came, naturally enough, it was a reprieve from the death sentence. There was no question of her receiving a full pardon for her crime, having a retrial or of course being released. It is completely untrue to state *"she had been released on the grounds that her crime was an act of desperation"*. This was not the case and nowhere was it reported to be the case. Overleaf are extracts from a representative sample of the many newspaper accounts.

"REPRIEVE. - The Home Secretary has granted a reprieve in the case of Alice Cleaver, . . . who is in Holloway Gaol under sentence of death for the murder of her baby . . . by throwing it out of a carriage window on the North London Railway near Dalston Junction." (The Times, March 15th 1909)

"The Home Secretary has advised the King to reprieve Alice Cleaver, . . . who was sentenced to death at the Old Bailey for the murder of her infant son by throwing him out of a railway carriage window at Dalston. Mr E.R.H. Blackwell one of the assistant undersecretaries of the Home Office, wrote to one of the girl's relatives announcing the decision."
(News of the World, March 21st 1909)

"Tottenham Murder Charge - Alice Cleaver . . . . " "The jury, however, after a short deliberation, found the woman guilty, with a strong recommendation to mercy.- Sentence of death was passed, ... It was notified on Wednesday that the Home Secretary had granted a reprieve." (Hornsey Journal, March 19th 1909)

"Murderer Reprieved
The Home Secretary has granted a reprieve in the case of Alice Cleaver . . . in Holloway Gaol under sentence of death for the murder of her baby . . . . "
(Weekly Herald, Tottenham & Edmonton, March 19th 1909)

Could it just be that Mr Lynch might not understand the language of the time, or indeed the subject ? But if this is the case, if he truly does not understand the meaning of the word reprieve, then it is I feel doubtful whether he should interpret and write on such a matter.

Having consulted a variety of dictionaries, all define reprieve in connection with the capital (death) sentence, describing it as a suspension, delay, remission or cancellation of the execution of a condemned person. Had he, to use a phrase well liked by political commentators at the time of elections, asked the man on the Clapham omnibus, he would have been told that *reprieve* meant just that. Many doubtless recalling, in the days before the abolition of the death penalty, the agonising wait that took place in the hours leading up to an execution. Wondering whether a reprieve would be granted, and if so knowing it would be replaced with life imprisonment.

On the other hand, there is no evidence to suggest Mr Lynch really mistook *reprieved* to mean *"released"* and I do not believe that he did. It is abundantly clear from the newspapers that the reprieve was granted only a few days after the death sentence. Therefore, in my view, the word *"eventually"* (as he applies it to her release), as opposed to *soon after* or *within a short time,* can only have been used as an indication that her release took place sometime within the next three years, to account for her being on the *Titanic* in April 1912, when of course she was not.

This leads us back to where we started, that Mr Lynch makes the statements he does concerning the release and on which his whole case rests. Yet when asked he has been unwilling to produce the slightest shred of evidence to support these statements, or give any reason for making them in the first place.

Why he went ahead and came to the conclusions he did, (unless severely flawed research and poor interpretation of the records can be held entirely responsible), perhaps I shall never know. But in the totally untrue story of Nurse Cleaver murdering a child he built the foundations for everything else he has then written about her. These lesser charges are considered in their own right on the following pages.

Before I leave this chapter I have one remaining observation, something that did not strike home at the time when I was so determinedly seeking confirmation of the release date. So sure was I that this could not have occurred prior to the *Titanic* tragedy that perhaps the most frightening aspect, the thought - what if by some strange twist of fate the perpetrator of the crime was alive and free in April 1912 - did not fully impact on me. Had this been the case, how could I so conclusively prove my mother's innocence - when no one thought it necessary to prove her guilt ?

8

The Lesser Charges

In addition to the murder charge, now dismissed, my mother, Nurse Cleaver, was supposedly guilty of:-

Obtaining Employment as a Nursemaid
by Deception

Responsibility for Death of a Family

Keeping Control of a Baby
in an Attempt to Afford herself Protection and Gain
Financial Advantage

Concealing her True Identity to Hide her Past

Being of an Unprepossessing Appearance

Taking Part in Attempted Extortion

8a

Inexperience ?

"When Alice Cleaver arrived in the first-class staterooms of her employers, the Hudson J.C. Allisons of Montreal, she was nervous yet excited. She had never imagined that one day she would be traveling across the ocean in such luxurious surroundings."

This is the innocent way in which my mother is first introduced to the reader in Mr Lynch's work. The forerunner of what is to come, combining a mixture of conjecture and statements which could apply equally as well to most on board.

There could have been few passengers or crew who weren't either in some way *"nervous"* or *"excited"*, perhaps both. Few who could have imagined they *"would be traveling across the ocean in such luxurious surroundings"*, when the *Titanic's* superiority to all her predecessors *was* and *is* well established. Furthermore, children's nursemaids, by their very role, were not unaccustomed to working and living in surroundings far above their own station in life.

~~~~~

From here we are quickly led into a rather less innocuous account -

"As nurse to the two Allison children, Alice Cleaver had much to conceal. Already her lack of experience was becoming obvious. Mrs. Allison often had to repeat instructions and assist in caring for the two children. But inexperience was not Alice's most important secret. Three years earlier she had murdered her own baby son."

The allegation, no the statement, is that Nurse Cleaver took a post with the Allisons, hiding not only her past as a child murderer but her inexperience, thus obtaining employment by deception. It has already been proven that she was not a child murderer, and neither had she borne an illegitimate child as is also put forward. Society has changed a great deal over the last ninety years, and is no longer upset or shocked by unmarried motherhood. However, you don't have to think back very far to appreciate what a serious assertion this is in its own right. My mother would have been terribly upset by this suggestion alone.

There was *nothing*, let alone *"much to conceal."*

This leaves only inexperience and ineptitude to answer for - but how do we know Mrs Allison found her employee so unsatisfactory ? Only through the author of course. Was he present during these 1912 exchanges ? He has not provided any source for his remarks - how else could he know ? It is very wrong to suggest there were any problems or friction when none existed. I think Mr and Mrs Allison would be horrified at the way their nursemaid has been treated, and this is not based upon false assumption and conjecture, but on the respect with which my mother spoke of her employers.

Having then gone on to acquaint us with details of the main charge, Mr Lynch, almost as if he feels further emphasis of inexperience, guilt and deception is necessary, continues -

"The Allisons' trained nurse had quit only a few weeks before sailing, and Alice had been hired in haste. If even a hint of her past slipped out, she would be unemployed and back on the Southampton docks with no hope of making a new life in Canada."

74

But Nurse Cleaver *was* a fully trained and experienced children's nurse. Would the Allisons really have taken such little care that they *"hired in haste"*, rather than at short notice, staff to look after their children ?

Whatever my mother's thoughts as she contemplated the voyage ahead, I can guarantee they bore no resemblance to the absurd images this conjures up. She could have had no thoughts of being ejected from the Allisons' suite and turned off the *Titanic "if even a hint of her past slipped out"*, or left standing jobless and forlorn as the departing vessel put to sea. No thoughts like these, because she had no past to slip out.

Should not the very fact of Nurse Cleaver's employment by the Allisons have indicated something amiss with the murder theory ? Is it likely that anyone of their standing would have employed a nursemaid without impeccable credentials and references ? Failing even to look into her background, and so taking on a laundress and convicted murderess, recently out of prison, instead of a bona fide nurse. Is this not just as much a slur on them ? Mr Allison, an astute businessman, Canadian financier and self-made millionaire, could afford the best in childcare and the best is what he got !

8b

Leaving the Titanic

So much criticism has recently been levelled at my mother, Nurse Cleaver, for her actions on the night of 14th/15th April 1912. At the time she was justly seen as a heroine, but in the rewriting of history, and dismissal of the previously established facts, she has become the villain. I ask you to lay aside all emotion and look at this situation in a rational and objective way and I will endeavour, as far as is possible, to do the same.

My mother had been engaged as a nursemaid to look after the two Allison children - Lorraine, nearly three years old, and baby Trevor. Mrs Allison had with her on the *Titanic* her maid, Sarah Daniels. As a lady's maid, Sarah Daniels' duties were to look after the needs of Mrs Allison. To take care of her possessions, in particular her dresses and jewellery, assist her lady in dressing and undressing, brushing and arranging her hair, preparing her bathwater and all the other little personal attentions.

Whilst I have no wish to enter into judgement on anyone aboard the *Titanic* that night, the actions of my mother, Nurse Cleaver, and the maid, Sarah Daniels, have been so strongly linked and their supposed motives contrasted, that I have little choice but to continue to refer to the latter. Otherwise it would necessitate skirting around the issue, therefore abandoning my quest to fully investigate this episode. It is simply not possible to consider the story, as it relates to my mother, without also referring to the maid.

I do not concur with Mr Lynch's account of Sarah Daniels taking the lead in twice waking an angry Mr Allison, and when asked he has not produced anything to back this up. On the second occasion we are told of her concern that *"her employer was not likely to be pleased at being awakened a second time"* and indeed, how on *"trying to convince him there was something seriously amiss. Instead he became cross with her for disturbing him and his wife."* On returning to her room to dress, apparently *"her roommate, Alice Cleaver, was reluctant to wake the sleeping baby, Trevor, so Sarah quickly pulled a fur-lined overcoat over her clothing and left on her own."*

Twice we are told, whilst making her way to the deck, of how she wished to return to warn her party. How her protestations against being ordered on deck and placed in a lifeboat were swept aside, with assurances that the Allisons would be taken care of. How, reassured, she entered boat No. 8.

We are asked to believe that the Allisons returned to sleep for a third time, and that Mr Allison, a responsible husband and father, did not at this stage have the sense to check if anything was untoward. Mr Lynch later stating - *"Hudson Allison had finally realized something was gravely wrong, and he went out to investigate. Leaving Alice Cleaver with his wife, Bess, and the two children, he headed for the upper decks."*

Before continuing, referring back to Sarah Daniels' departure, I ask just one question - why should the nurse have woken the baby ? Maybe it only serves to highlight the difference between how this maid and the calm, experienced Nurse Cleaver would and did react. What purpose would it have served for the nurse-maid to have deliberately woken her charge, an eleven-month-old baby, turning him from a peaceful sleeping infant, unaware of any danger, into a fractious, frightened child ?

I do not dispute that Mr Allison did go to make enquiries, leaving the nurse to help his wife, that Sarah Daniels did dress, leave on her own and go up on deck. She then entered a lifeboat.

She may or may not have had intentions of returning to the family, she may or may not have protested against entering a lifeboat (all this conjecture unless Mr Lynch can produce documentation). Neither do there appear to be any independent eyewitness accounts of her actions that night. The only reports I have seen in the newspapers point to her, or those she is said to have contacted, as the source. From the latter it appears not only did she leave on one of the last lifeboats, instead of one of the first, but she was the baby's saviour. The child being handed to her on the deck of the *Titanic* by his mother, who refused to leave her husband.* Surprisingly not even the existence of a nurse is mentioned in these. Should we believe these newspaper accounts, which would seem to directly contradict Mr Lynch's own statements ? * See Page 127

To continue - *"Alice found Bess Allison nearly hysterical and trying to dress. She helped her employer put on a blouse and petticoat, then a fur coat. She then buttoned up her shoes and set out some brandy. Two-year-old Loraine and baby Trevor were still sleeping. Just as Mrs. Allison was beginning to calm down a little, a steward came by and ordered everyone up on deck. Now both women began to panic."*

The last sentence is particularly interesting coming from someone who never met my mother, and presumably was not present on the *Titanic* that night. Never once have I known my mother to panic, whatever the situation she was faced with, whether the emergency be large or small. As far as I am concerned, if my mother was anything to go by, the word panic has never appeared within the vocabulary of the true British Nanny.

Then *"With Bess Allison once again verging on hysterics and still no sign of either Mr. Allison or Sarah Daniels, Alice was faced with rescuing a distraught mother and two tiny children all by herself. In fear for her own safety, she quickly grabbed a fur rug . . . wrapped it over the baby's nightgown, and announced to Mrs. Allison that she would not let the child out of her arms. Then, before the distraught mother could stop her, Alice took the baby and disappeared. As Alice hurried along the hallway, she passed Mr. Allison on his way back to his stateroom."*

There are of course no eyewitnesses to this supposed child snatching. Here, as with everything else, we have to rely on the author of these words, who once again has remarkable insight into events that took place so many years ago, between parties unable to testify to the real truth. Why the nurse would wish, as insinuated, to snatch the child, or how this relates to her own safety is left unexplained. What would be the purpose behind it ?

Finally, he ends his narrative of her deeds aboard the *Titanic* with a description of her arrival at, and climbing into, lifeboat 11 - having passed the baby to a crew member, who was then permitted to follow her.

~~~~~

Returning briefly to the maid's behaviour, all that can be said is that she left before she had carried out her duty to her lady. Mr Lynch himself acknowledges this in pointing out that Mrs Allison was not even dressed at the time.

The nurse surely had enough to do in respect of the two young children, without having to take over the duties of a lady's maid and help Mrs Allison so much. If there was no onus on the maid to look after her lady, why was she travelling first class, on hand for the Allisons - why was she not in second class with the cook and the chauffeur, whose services were not required during the voyage ? Yet by Mr Lynch's own admission, not only did the inexperienced and ineffectual nurse he earlier depicted, calm down the hysterical mother, but dressed her and gave her brandy. She then prepared baby Trevor for the harsh conditions ahead and, I believe, also took equal care with preparations for little Lorraine as her mother was obviously in no fit state to do so.

Unlike her fellow servant, who receives no criticism, Nurse Cleaver did not dress and leave on her own without telling any of the family. If she had been *"in fear for her own safety"* she could have left at any time, without the unnecessary encumbrance of a small baby. She may well have promised Mrs Allison *"that she would not let the child out of her arms"*, as was her duty. She certainly did not take the baby and disappear, both parents were

79

well aware that she had him safely, Mr Allison returning to the stateroom as she left.

We are told *"a steward came by and ordered everyone up on deck."* Each steward and stewardess had responsibility for a specific number of rooms and their occupants in the case of an emergency. This responsibility extended to ensuring passengers left their rooms (which were then locked), and made their way to the lifeboats. More than that they could not do. Obviously this procedure was not entirely successful, but it is well documented that Lorraine Allison was the only child in first or second class to die, and Mrs Allison one of only four first-class women passengers to be lost. She along with two others choosing not to be parted from their husbands - the fourth being unaccounted for.

Bearing in mind their responsibilities, and Mr Lynch's words, the stewards must have been present when Mrs Allison determined to wait with Lorraine for her husband's imminent return, and when she allowed the nurse to start for the decks with the baby. It would be as unfair to suggest that they left Mrs Allison on her own, or indeed allowed the nurse to make off with the child, as it is untrue to claim that Nurse Cleaver did anything other than abide by the wishes and instructions of her mistress - and orders of the stewards.

It was only reasonable and logical that the nurse would take care of the baby, and the parents the daughter. There is no evidence that either party objected to this arrangement, with both parents present and under such unusual circumstances, it would have only been proper. Other reports have noted the difficulties passengers faced in trying to leave the ship, being sent from deck to deck, having to negotiate awkward stairways and of course climb into lifeboats.

Whether the Allisons did or did not immediately follow their nurse and child as far as the boat deck, and if not why not - none can tell - only they knew the answer to that. Why did they lag behind ? Maybe Mrs Allison still needed encouragement, and possibly the party went in different directions. How much anxiety this separation caused them we do not know, but the person who doubts an innocent separation must be that rare specimen, someone who has never once become parted from their friends or family whilst on an outing. In the calm, uneventful, mundane world the friends you thought were right behind you are not there, they have been momentarily distracted, and you are alone. Remember that embarrassing moment in a crowded shop when you speak to the relative standing next to you, only to find you are addressing a stranger. All who judge, scoff and dismiss are surely superior to the rest of us. When you and your child have become separated, is this through evil intent on your part, or theirs ? If when this happens they are accompanied by a friend, relation, or even a nanny, should some sinister motive instantly be placed on it ? To appreciate the true situation -

Firstly, remove this occurrence from that of everyday life and place it in the midst of a disaster. Imagine the sheer size of the *Titanic*, which many of those most directly involved felt the public did not fully appreciate. In their books collected together in *The Story of the Titanic as Told by its Survivors* - Lightoller (the senior surviving officer), expresses the problems of trying *"to convey any idea of the size of a ship like the Titanic"*; Lawrence Beesley (a second-class passenger), notes the *Titanic* as being *"a sixth of a mile long"* and refers to the chances of becoming lost. This, all before the night of 14th/15th April. Now picture this on that fateful night - Archibald Gracie (a first-class passenger), also refers to the ship's size and length, and trying to explain this to friends. But perhaps more to the point, he relates the story of at least one passenger becoming separated *"in the crowd"* (in this case from her sisters) - without doubt not the only incident of its kind.* Beesley too continually mentions *"the crowd"* on the decks.

* Some mothers are said to have found themselves temporarily leaving a child behind on the ship.

Secondly, try to remove from your mind the totally false knowledge, previously imparted to many of you, portraying my mother as a volatile murderess. No longer consider her actions in this light. Look at her instead the way Mr and Mrs Allison did, as a reputable experienced nursemaid, someone they had carefully chosen and to whom they had entrusted their two children. Someone who took charge in an emergency, calmed and prepared

Mrs Allison and her children, fulfilling Mr Allison's faith in leaving her to do just that. Again, by Mr Lynch's own admission, as the husband returned to the stateroom his wife and children were ready to leave, and who had got them ready - the Nurse.

~~~~~

On reaching the boat deck Mr Allison, along with the other male passengers, would either have been refused entry to a life-boat, or had to wait until there were no more women and children to come, depending on how the officer concerned interpreted - *Women and Children First.*

Before Mr Lynch's book there was general consensus that Mrs Allison refused to leave without her husband, as other women refused to leave without theirs. It must be remembered that many people did not believe the *Titanic* would sink, and many husbands doubted the wisdom of placing their wives and children in the boats, believing they stood a better chance by remaining on board the *Titanic.* Therefore, in all probability Mr Allison did not sufficiently force his wife and daughter to leave until it was too late for both of them.

The implied reason by Lynch is that Mrs Allison failed to leave because she did not know what had happened to her baby. This is to imply also, that whilst they were not prepared to leave the sinking ship, without knowing their son to be safe, at the same time they were prepared to sacrifice their daughter. This does a great injustice to the Allisons who surely would have secured their daughter's safety, had they appreciated the true situation, by placing her in a lifeboat in the care of a responsible passenger.

It makes no sense at all, for even had the nurse really grabbed the baby and left, there was only one direction in which she would have been heading - the lifeboats ! After all Mr Lynch recounts that that is exactly where she did go. In what other direction would she have been likely to go - the bowels of the ship ? Yet there were no accounts by officers, or others, manning the lifeboat stations, of the desperate parents rushing from one lifeboat to another asking whether their baby had been seen.

Mrs Allison's refusal to leave the ship without her husband is not just a matter of pure speculation on my part, but the impartial truth as related by eyewitnesses. Colonel Archibald Gracie, himself a survivor, widely acknowledged as a most reliable and truthful amateur historian, who diligently researched and provided a contemporary 1912 account of the disaster in his book, *The Truth about the Titanic* (now published as *Titanic, A Survivor's Story*), had the following to say about Mrs H J Allison of Montreal -

"Mrs. Allison and Miss Allison could have been saved had they not chosen to remain on the ship. They refused to enter the lifeboat unless Mr. Allison was allowed to go with them. This statement was made in my presence by Mrs. H.A. Cassobeer, of New York, who related it to Mrs. Allison's [*] brother, Mr. G.F. Johnston, and myself." * Mrs Allison senior - Hudson's mother.

No mention here of baby Trevor's supposed disappearance having any part in Mrs Allison's refusal to leave the Titanic, only the fact that she wouldn't leave her husband. Colonel Gracie then continues, referring also to another first class passenger who refused to be parted from her husband -

"Those of us who survived among the first cabin passengers will remember this beautiful Mrs. Allison, and will be glad to know of the heroic mould in which she was cast, as exemplified by her fate, which was similar to that of another, Mrs. Straus, who has been memorialized the world over."

In *A Night to Remember* Walter Lord states -

"No amount of persuasion or force could move Mrs. Hudson J. Allison of Montreal. A little apart from the rest, she huddled close to Mr. Allison. Their baby Trevor had gone in a boat with the nurse, but Lorraine, their three-year-old daughter, still tugged at her mother's skirt."

Later reporting how -

"The Allisons stood smiling on the Promenade Deck, Mrs. Allison grasping little Lorraine with one hand, her husband with the other."

Mr Lord therefore concurring with the Colonel's account, that Mrs Allison's refusal to leave was because she would not be parted from her husband.

It is curious how both of these authorities are cited in Mr Lynch's bibliography, but neither worthy of consideration when it comes to his account of the Allisons. This despite his recorded high opinion of the Colonel's book.

Some may quote Major Peuchen and refer to his witnessing the last moments of Mrs Allison, but they would have to be selective in their quotes. If the newspapers are to be believed, on the *Titanic* he was here, there and everywhere, and on reaching New York gave an interview to just about every Canadian paper possible. I have seen a different account attributed to Major Peuchen for at least every day of the week, if not every day of the month. The majority state that Mrs Allison died a heroine's death, steadfastly refusing to save herself without her husband; some refer to her and her husband becoming separated; the odd one even mentions her being distracted about her baby; many more report that she had put the nurse and baby into a lifeboat and some suggest she left them on being told her husband was in a boat on the opposite side of the *Titanic*.

Major Peuchen is also credited with waking the Allisons, escorting the nurse and baby off the *Carpathia* and locating the child's relatives, to whom he recounted the last moments of Mr and Mrs Allison. Although leaving comparatively early in lifeboat No. 6, on the instructions of Second Officer Lightoller, some quote him as witnessing the last moments of Mrs Allison; how she fell into the water from a submerged raft, her body floating back to those of her husband and child; or, she entered a collapsible boat and was standing up to her knees in water when last seen - he thought her daughter was with her; or, that the last he saw was little Lorraine running to a sailor by the then partially submerged ship's rail, before being brought back by her parents.

No doubt Mrs Allison *was* concerned for her baby, but reference to being distracted is not accompanied by any suggestion that this was because she was ignorant of his whereabouts or safety. Neither, in the accounts seen, is this given as a reason for her not leaving the *Titanic*. According to Major Peuchen, if the newspapers are to be believed, she informed him that she had been advised to leave, but would not do so. Mr Allison telling him that he had urged her to go - on neither occasion was a missing or absent child mentioned as the reason she would not.

~~~~~

Later in his book, after the survivors reach New York, Mr Lynch again returns to the subject of leaving the *Titanic*, this time to put forward supposed views of Mr and Mrs Allisons' families, yet more unfounded statements -

"However, the families of Hudson and Bess Allison saw nothing heroic in Miss Cleaver's behavior. They believed the nurse had panicked when she rushed on deck with Trevor, leaving Mrs. Allison in an impossible situation. She was not the type of woman to leave the ship without first knowing with absolute certainty that her baby was safe. They held Alice Cleaver indirectly responsible for the deaths of Bess, Hudson, and their daughter, Loraine. Mrs. Allison's mother would long be haunted by the idea that it could just as easily have been Hudson Allison rather than Steward William Faulkner who stepped into lifeboat No. 11 with Trevor in his arms."

This is where the mysterious *"they"* comes into play - *"they believed"* and *"they held"*. The truth of these general, and on request, still unsubstantiated references to *"the families"* can, I think, be seen by referring to the truth of the author's other statements regarding my mother. We are urged to believe and hold that the Allisons thought Nurse Cleaver responsible for the

85

deaths of Hudson, Bess and Lorraine. Urged to believe by the same person who in one breath tells us that Mrs Allison hastily appointed a convicted murderer as her son's nanny, and next - *"she was not the type of woman to leave the ship without first knowing with absolute certainty that her baby was safe"* - somewhat contradictory. I *believe* the Allisons did hold my mother greatly accountable for one thing, that *"they believed"* her directly responsible for one thing - the saving of baby Trevor's life !

If indeed Mrs Allison's mother (Mrs Sarah Daniels) did feel any resentment towards the nurse, surely this would be no more than that she felt towards her daughter's personal maid - why ? Because they survived, and her daughter Bess did not.

In times of tragedy most look for an answer, or a reason, for something which is so hard to accept - many for someone to blame. It is a natural human reaction. To ask any parent to see things entirely rationally, when faced with such a terrible outcome, is not realistic. He declares Mrs Allison's mother long held the view that her son-in-law would otherwise have been granted a place in the lifeboats, a clearly irrational view in the face of what we all know through well-documented sources. Mr Lynch does not state he agrees with this view, nor could he with his knowledge of what went on at the lifeboat stations. I question the necessity of reporting Mrs Daniels' alleged views which, but for her grief, would be most unreasonable towards the nurse who saved her grandson and less than thoughtful towards the young crewman and his family.

Had the whole party been together beside a lifeboat, rather than just the couple and their daughter, it is extremely doubtful that Mr Allison would have been allowed to occupy the space taken by one of the crew, else why were so many other husbands and wives, fathers and children separated. So many men were refused entry to the boats, some women literally being wrenched from their husbands to be saved.

But if Mrs Daniels did imply that someone else took the place Mr Allison might indeed *should* have had, thereby making this an all-important factor, here once again we return to the crux of the matter - recognition that without her husband, Mrs Allison would not leave.

From the moment the nurse left their rooms with Trevor, Mr Lynch's interest in the Allisons on board the *Titanic* appears to cease, despite him taking the trouble to get the reader interested in their plight. Instead we, having had the ideas firmly planted in our minds, are left to assume the worst by combining earlier highly inaccurate representation of events and his subsequent remarks about the families. The author missing out what happened once the Allisons reached the decks, and what decisions they took. How unique, a story of *Titanic* victims confined to below decks - when they were not.

At the risk of repeating myself, I do not believe the Allisons held such concern for their baby boy and yet at the same time were willing to sacrifice their daughter. With hindsight we all know the *Titanic* was sinking fast, but how many of the people on board that night really appreciated the gravity of the situation until it was too late ?

How many felt like Washington Dodge, who stated in his address to the Commonwealth Club in San Francisco - *"I myself, hesitated to place my wife and child in this boat,* [lifeboat No. 1] *being unable to decide whether it would be safer to keep them on the steamer, or to entrust them to this frail boat, which was the first to be launched, and which hung over eighty feet above the water."* Then, describing his family's departure - *"As I saw this boat lowered, containing my wife and child, I was overwhelmed with doubts, as to whether or not I was exposing them to greater danger, than if they had remained on board the ship."*

Shortly afterwards noting how - *"Many expressed their determination to take their chances with the steamer rather than embark in the lifeboats. This unusual circumstance may be accounted for by the fact that the officers had insisted that under the worst conditions possible, the "Titanic" could not sink in less than eight or ten hours, and that a number of steamers had been communicated with by wireless, and would be standing by to offer relief within an hour or two."*

Dr Dodge was clearly not alone in these thoughts, and in his address refers to other husbands who held exactly the same fears for their wives and children. There is no reason to think that the Allisons felt any differently from other passengers. But the refusal of Mrs Allison to leave without her husband, and who can blame her for any additional fears she might have had when viewing the drop of the boats to the water below, was, for her and her daughter, the deciding factor.   By the time the true situation became apparent to many of the passengers, it was too late, the boats had gone !

~~~~~

In conclusion, I leave you to consider whether someone who has totally inaccurately identified an innocent woman as a child murderer, can now be regarded as accurate in his further portrayal of that same individual. Portrayal in the light of which can hardly be said to be objective as he was under such a false impression.

For anyone to suggest that my mother, Nurse Cleaver, after all the assistance she gave, was in any way responsible for the deaths of the Allisons is unforgivable. This to my mind is also to suggest that the Allisons were incompetent adults, had no control over their destiny, were unable to make their own decisions - in short that their fate lay in the hands of their nursemaid.

If a murder charge can be asserted without realising any burden of proof, then has Mr Lynch been more careful in forming his later opinions or interpreting such records that he *may* have to hand ?

He seems to think he knew my mother's thoughts and actions on leaving the *Titanic.* But did he not presume also to know them when describing how she somehow looked back on a secret past (that did not exist) on leaving Southampton ?

8c

The Carpathia to New York

It seems that my mother, Nurse Cleaver's cardinal sin on board the *Carpathia* was that she, Trevor Allison's nursemaid, would not allow the baby to be given up to the lady's maid, Sarah Daniels. Bearing in mind how it has previously been stressed by her accuser that, on leaving Mrs Allison, she promised *she would not let the child out of her arms"* it is I feel, not for the first time, somewhat contradictory to blame her for sticking to her word, and indeed her duty. Whilst Sarah Daniels may have felt excused from assisting Mrs Allison on board the *Titanic*, my mother would not have felt excused from her duty to the baby, and would not have taken it upon herself to hand her charge over to another. Despite this Mr Lynch cannot refrain from notifying us that -

"One unattractive scene was played repeatedly during the voyage to New York. Nurse Alice Cleaver refused to allow Sarah Daniels near little Trevor Allison, the only member of the Allison family to survive the sinking, even when he would cry out and stretch his arms toward Sarah."

But where is the evidence of such dramatic scenes as are suggested between the Allison servants on board the *Carpathia*?

The day before they reached New York, Mildred Brown, the cook, wrote a letter home (British Titanic Society - *Atlantic Daily Bulletin* - Vol 3/1995). In which she referred to Sarah Daniels, remarking *"I found Sallie had got on alright but poor girl she keeps worrying about her things . . . . "* No mention here of the maid being upset by the nurse, or of such public conflict between these two servants, which we are told took place *"repeatedly"*.

However, I know, in my mother's situation, I would not have felt very kindly towards someone who did not remain long enough even to help her lady in dressing but left me to do this in addition to caring for the two young children. Nor could I have put aside the thought - had Miss Daniels remained, she as Mrs Allison's personal maid, would surely have had a greater chance of persuading her mistress to leave, or at least give up Lorraine to the pair of us. Without a clinging wife and child, Mr Allison too would have had a greater chance of survival. Lightoller and young Thayer are examples of those who successfully jumped for their lives at the last moment. Or indeed there may have been a possibility, like Washington Dodge, of finding a place in the boats after his wife and child had left.

Be that as it may, Sarah Daniels did not remain, but once the remnants of the Allison party reached the *Carpathia*, we are expected to believe that she deserved some special rights, of a type not usually accorded to a lady's maid, in respect of the child. We are to forget that those were the days when servants' roles were well and truly defined, and each would have been aware of their own place and duties.

Would that I had not been forced to return to the subject of Miss Daniels, this time aboard the *Carpathia*, but she has been set up as some kind of heroine, a tool with which to further blacken my mother's name. Had she not been used in such a way as to portray good against evil I would have no need to do so. On board the *Titanic* Sarah Daniels, her part in these events so conveniently glossed over, has been excused for leaving, whilst my mother has been condemned though she stayed, helped the Allisons and saved their baby.

So far I have dealt with the allegation that Nurse Cleaver wouldn't let the maid near the child, but what of the following supposed reasons for this action ?

"No doubt she saw the Allison baby as some sort of insurance: as long as she had him in her clutches, she was safe. As the child's savior, perhaps she could even work this to her financial advantage."

Is this conjecture to be taken as my mother's thoughts or just the imaginings of the author, again betraying his lack of knowledge of her ? That she was eager to keep hold of the child for her own purposes, and somehow to protect herself, is clearly stated. Quite how her safety depended on being in possession of the baby, or what he was an insurance against, is left unexplained as is the meaning of *"work this to her financial advantage."*

I can only ask you, the reader, what feelings you would have if your loved one, who throughout her life had only the concerns of others to heart, and was impeccable in her character, were so shamefully portrayed as some sort of evil schemer who did nothing, even to the extent of saving and caring for a child, without an ulterior motive.

That my mother was a bona fide nursemaid is indisputable, that she should retain sole control of her charge in the absence of any of his family is without question. Baby Trevor was not a parcel to be passed around the other servants. That she was entitled to receive wages for her duties as a nursemaid goes without saying, that she sought any more than this can only be pure fantasy. Knowing my mother as I did I have no hesitation in stating that nothing could be further from fact or reality than the declaration *"no doubt she saw . . . advantage."* I maintain it has no foundation in truth whatsoever. Despite our request to the author this allegation remains unsubstantiated.

The truth is that so well did she care for her charge, known to be a delicate baby, not only did he suffer no lasting ill effects from spending hours in a lifeboat in such freezing conditions, but slept right through the entire ordeal.

The next three days, during which the *Carpathia* made her way back to New York, must have seemed an eternity both for those on board and those around the globe anxiously awaiting news of their friends and relatives. But, little as they may have appreciated it at the time, this period of isolation from the rest of the world was probably a godsend for the survivors. A pause between the noise, bustle and high spirits of the evening of 14th April, swiftly followed by scenes of unimaginable horror that night, and the overwhelming media attention with which they were to be met on arrival at New York on 18th April.

During this time the *Carpathia*, in spite of the numbers she now accommodated, must have been an unusually quiet, contemplative place, both for the survivors and her own crew and passengers, whose scheduled voyage had been interrupted. Shock, grief and compassion meant she could be little else. A few still held out hope that they would be reunited with those who had not found their way from the *Titanic* to the *Carpathia*, but might by some other means have been saved. Ultimately this would serve only to delay the inevitable acceptance of their loss.

Yet, many miles away events were unfolding, which eighty years later would be produced and used against my mother. The press on both sides of the Atlantic were ravenous in their coverage of the disaster, and among the newspaper articles starting to appear were the lists of survivors and those lost.

Many of these lists were inaccurate, giving false hope and despair in equal measure. Over the days that followed they were continually amended as more information reached land, and by the time the *Carpathia* arrived at New York a clearer, although not completely accurate, picture had emerged.

The following pages show extracts from some of the American, in particular New York, newspapers covering the entries for my mother, Nurse Cleaver (the Allison nurse). From these it can be seen how some papers, at least as regards her, had established the situation clearly from the first, whilst others took a day or two to catch up.

IC SINKS FOUR HOURS AFTER HITTING ICEBE
RESCUED BY CARPATHIA, PROBABLY 1250 PE
Y SAFE, MRS. ASTOR MAYBE, NOTED NAMES M

The Lost Titanic Being Towed Out of Belfast Harbor.

CAPT. E. J. SMITH,
Commander of the Titanic.

PARTIAL LIST OF THE SAVED.

Includes Bruce Ismay, Mrs. Widener, Mrs. H. B. Harris, and an Incomplete name, suggesting Mrs. Astor's.

Special to The New York Times.

CAPE RACE, N. F., Tuesday, April 16.—Following is a partial list of survivors among the first-class passengers of the Titanic, received by the Marconi wireless station this morning, from the Carpathia, via the steamship Olympic:

Mrs. JACOB P. —— and maid.
Mr. HARRY ANDERSON.
Mrs. ED. W. APPLETON.
Mrs. ROSE ABBOTT.
Miss G. M. BURNS.
Miss D. D. CASSEBERE.
Mrs. WM. M. CLARKE.
Mrs. B. CHIBINACE.
Miss E. G. CROSSBIE.
Miss H. ROSEBIE.
Miss JEAN HIPACK.
Mrs. HY. B. HARRIS.
Mrs. ALEX. HALVERSON.
Miss MARGARET BAYS.
Mr. BRUCE ISMAY.
Mr. and Mrs. ED. KIMBERLEY.
Mr. F. A. KENNYMAN.
Miss EMILE KENCHEN.
Miss G. F. LONGLEY.
Mrs. A. F. LEADER.
Miss BERTHA LAVORY.
Mrs. ERNEST LIVES.
Miss MARY CLINES.
Mrs. SINGRID LINDSTROM.
Mr. GUSTAVE J. LESNEUR.
Miss GIORGETTA A. MADILL.
Mme. MELICARD.
Mrs. TUCKER and maid.
Mrs. J. B. THAYER.
Mr. J. B. THAYER, Jr.
Mr. HENRY WOOLMER.
Miss ANNA WARD.
Mr. RICHARD M. WILLIAMS.
Mrs. F. M. WARNER.
Miss HELEN A. WILSON.
Miss WILLARD.
Miss MARY WICKS.
Mrs. GEO. D. WIDENER and maid.
Mrs. J. STEWART WHITE.
Miss MARIE YOUNG.
Mrs. THOMAS POTTER, Jr.
Mrs. EDNA S. ROBERTS.
Countess of ROTHES.

Mr. C. ROLMANE.
Mrs. SUSAN P. ROGERSON. (Probably Ryerson).
Miss EMILY B. ROGERSON.
Mrs. ARTHUR ROGERSON.
Master ALLISON and nurse.
Miss K. T. ANDREWS.
Miss NINETTE PANHART.
Miss E. W. ALLEN.
Mr. and Mrs. D. BISHOP.
Mr. H. BLANK.
Miss A. BASSINA.
Mrs. JAMES BAXTER.
Mr. GEORGE A. BAYTO—
Miss C. BONNELL.
Mrs. J. M. BROWN.
Miss G. C. BOWEN.
Mr. and Mrs. R. L. BECKW—
Miss RUTH TAUSSIG.
Miss ELLA THOR.
Mr. and Mrs. E. Z. TAYLOR.
GILBERT M. TUCKER.
Mr. J. B. THAYER.
Mr. JOHN B. ROGERSON.
Mrs. M. ROTHSCHILD.
Miss MADELEINE NEWELL.
Mrs. MARJORIE NEWELL.
HELEN W. NEWSOM.
Mrs. FIENNAD OMOND.
Mr. E. C. OSTBY.
Miss HELEN R. OSTBY.
Mrs. MAMAM J. REYAGO.
Mlle. OLIVIA.
Mrs. D. W. MERVIN.
Mr. PHILIP EMOCK.
Mr. JAMES GOOGHT.
Miss RUBERTA MAIMY.
Mr. PIERRE MARECHAL.
Mrs. W. E. MINEHAN.
Miss APPIE RANELT.
Major ARTUR PEUCHEN.
Mrs. KARL H. BEHR.
Miss DESSETTE.

Mrs. WILLIAM BUCKNELL.
Mrs. O. H. BARKWORTH.
Mrs. H. B. STEFFASON.
Mrs. ELSIE BOWERMAN.

The Marconi station reports that it missed the word after "Mrs. Jacob P." In a list received by the Associated Press this morning this name appeared well down, but in THE TIMES list it is first, suggesting that the name of Mrs. John Jacob Astor is intended. This supposition is strengthened by the fact that, except for Mrs. H. J. Allison, Mrs. Astor is the only lady in the "A" column of the ship's passenger list attended by a maid.

NAMES PICKED UP AT BOSTON.

BOSTON, April 15.—Among the names of survivors of the Titanic picked up by wireless from the steamer Carpathia here to-night were the following:

Mr. and Mrs. L. HENRY.
Mrs. W. A. HOOPER.
Mr. MILE.
Mr. J. FLYNN.
Miss ALICE FORTUNE.
Mrs. ROBERT DOUGLAS.
Miss HILDA SLAYTHI.
Mrs. P. SMITH.
Mrs. BRAHAM.
Miss LUCILLE CARTER.
Mr. WILLIAM CARTER.
Mrs. CUMMINGS.
Mrs. FLORENCE WARE.
Miss ALICE PHILLIPS.
Mrs. PAULA RUNGE.
Miss JANE ——.
Miss PHYLLIS O. ——.
HOWARD B. CASE.
Miss MINEHAN.
Miss BERTHA ——.

THE PROBABLE LOSS.
Number Aboard.
First cabin ....
Second cabin ....

LIST OF SURVIVORS' NAMES ONLY 400.

As Transmitted From the Carpathia By Way of the Olympic—Latter Was Still in Communication After List Sent—Anxious Waiting for Names That May Be Added.

The following list of passengers rescued from the Titanic and now being brought to this city on the steamship Carpathia contains all the names sent from the Carpathia. These names were sent through the Olympic and, as a dispatch to THE TIMES from Cape Race, printed elsewhere, points out, seemed to be all the Olympic had received from the Carpathia. What names the Carpathia may have to add cannot be known until the Carpathia is again heard from. Four hundred or more survivors remain to be accounted for. These, of course, include the members of the Titanic's crew who left the ship.

By comparing the names with those listed in the passenger list, it will be seen that some names appearing among the survivors were not contained on the passenger lists. These may have joined the ship at Cherbourg or Queenstown after the formal lists were made out. Only the purser of the Titanic would probably have record of these names. Such names are listed below in each of the various classes.

Occasionally in the list of survivors, some duplication will be found, owing to the uncertainty of spelling in transmission from the Carpathia.

[In the various forms they may fit.]

A.

Mrs. HANNAH ABELSON.
Mrs. MARJORIE COLLYER.
Mrs. ROSE ABBOTT, (probably Mrs. N. ABBOTT.)
Miss E. W. ALLEN.
Master ALLISON and nurse.
Miss GEORGETTA ANNADILL.
Mr. HARRY ANDERSON.
Miss K. T. ANDREWS, (probably Miss CORNELIA I. ANDREWS.)
Mr. and Mrs. WILLIAM ANGLE.
Mr. E. D. APPLETON.
Mr. GEORGE ARDEN.
Mrs. JOHN JACOB ASTOR and maid.

B.

ADA E. BALLS.
Mrs. A. H. BARKWORTH.
KARL BARRATT.
Miss A. BASSINA.
MIAH BATHWORTH.
Mrs. JAMES BAXTER.
Mr. GEORGE BRATTON.
Miss MARGARET BAYS.
EDWARD BEALE, or BEANE.
Mrs. ETHEL BEANE.
Mrs. ALLEN BECKER, or BEIKER.
RICHARD BECKER, probably BEIK-ER.
RUTH BECKER, probably BEIKER.
Miss MARY BECKER, or BEIKER.
Mr. and Mrs. R. I. BECKWITH.
Mr. KARL H. BEHR.
Miss LILLIAN BENTHAM.
Miss BESSETTE.
Miss DAGMAR BRIGHT, maybe Miss DAGMAR BRYL.
ALFRED DRACHENSTED.
LULU DREW.
Mrs. B. DRISCOLL.
Miss FLORENTINE DUVAN.
LENORA ASUNCION DURANTE.
Miss C. BENNELL, probably Miss C. BONNELL.
Mr. H. BLANK.
Mr. and Mrs. D. H. BISHOP.
Miss JEAN HIPPACH.
Mr. and Mrs. FRED M. HOYT.

Mrs. CHARLOTTE COLLIER.
W. HAMALANIAN.
Miss JENNIE HANSON.
MINNIE MALICROFT, may be CROFT.
Mrs. H. E. CROSSBIE.
Mrs. J. B. CUMMINGS.

D.

Miss SARAH DANIELS.
ROBERT W. DANIEL, H. HAREN.
Mrs. MARY DANZER.
Miss MARY DAVIDSON.
Mrs. THORNTON DAVIDSON.
JOHN DAVIES, may be CHARLES DAVIES.
Mrs. AGNES DAVIS.
Miss MARY DAVIS.
Miss DESSETTE, or BESSETTE.
Mme. B. DEVILLIERS.
Mr. and Mrs. A. A. DICK.
Mr. and Mrs. WASHINGTON DODGE and son.
Miss SARAH DODGE.
Mrs. ADA DOLING.
Miss ELSIE DOLING.
Mr. F. C. DOUGLAS.
Mrs. ROBERT DOUGLAS.
Mr. W. DOUGLAS.
Mrs. WALTER DOUGLAS.

H.

H. HAMALANIAN.
W. HAMALANIAN.
Mrs. FLORENCE MARE.
Mr. and Mrs. G. A. HARDER.
Mr. and Mrs. HENRY B. HARPER and servant.
NANCY HARPER, or NINA HAR-PER.
GEORGE HARRIS.
Mrs. HY. B. HARRIS.
Mrs. ESTHER HART and Miss EVA HART.
Mr. MASABUMI HOSENO.
Mr. HASSENS.
H. HAVEN.
W. J. HAWKSFORD.
Mrs. MARGARET HAYS.
Mr. and Mrs. CHARLES M. HAYS.
Miss NORA HEALY.
Mrs. ALICE HEARMAN.
Mrs. JANE HEARMAN.
Miss KATE HEARMAN.
Mr. and Mrs. L. HENRY.
Mrs. MARY HEWLETT.
Mr. and Mrs. JAMES HINON.
Mr. and Mrs. GEO. HOCKING.
Miss ELIZA HOCKING.
Miss NELLIE HOCKING.
Mr. J. C. HOGEBOOM.
Miss ANNA HOLD and Mr. STE-PHEN HOLD.
Mrs. ALEX HOLVERSON.
HENRY R. HOMER or H. R. HOR-NER.
H. HONONS.
Mrs. W. A. HOOPER.
Miss IDA S. HIPPACH.

M.

Miss MILLIE MALICROFT (proba-bly Miss NELLIE WALCROFT.)
JOHN MELORA.
Mr. MILE MILLET (probably FRANK D. MILLET.)
Mrs. W. E. MINAHAN.
Mrs. DAISY MINAHAN.
Mr. and Mrs. D. W. MERVIN or MARVIN.
Mrs. MULLINGER and child.
Mrs. PAULA MUNGE or Manga.
Mr. and Mrs. WASHINGTON NEW-ELL, or Miss MARJORIE NEW-ELL.
Miss MADELINE NEWELL.
HELEN M. NEWSOME.
Mrs. ELIZABETH NYE.
Mrs. NASSER.

D.

Miss R. O'CONNELL, probably Mrs. ROBERT C. CORNELL.
Mlle. OLIVIA.
Mr. FIELNAM OMOND.
Miss HELEN R. OSTBY.
Mr. and Mrs. E. OSTBY.
PERCY J. OXENHAM.
THOMAS OXENHAM.

Miss MILLIE MALICROFT (proba-bly Miss NELLIE WALCROFT.)
Mr. and Mrs. PAUL SCHABERT.
Miss EMMA SEGEBBEL.
Mrs. WALTER REELBERG.
Mrs. JESSIE W. SEITCH.
Mrs. AUGUSTA SEREPECA.
Mr. FREDERICK SEWARD.
ROBERT DOUGLAS SHEDDEL.
Miss SHUTER, (probably Miss E. W. SHUTES.
Col. ALFONSO SIMONT &. R. SPENCER SILVERTHORNE.
Mrs. L. SIMONE.
Miss L. SIMONS.
Miss MAUDE SINCOCK.
Mrs. W. M. SLOPER.
Mrs. HILDA SLATTER.
WILLIAM T. SLOPER.
Mrs. LUCIAN P. SMITH.
MARION SMITH.
Mrs. P. SMITH.
Mrs. L. FIMONE.
Mr. A. L. SALOMON.

OF SURVIVORS HAS NAMES OF ONL

MISS E. W. ALLEN.

MR. AND MRS. JOHN B. THAYER.

M. J. WHITE.

MR.

CARTER. MR. W. E. CARTER

BENJAMIN GUGGENHEIM.

J. CLINCH SMITH.

W. A. ROEBLING

monetary loss c night, although run into the mil

"We can repla "but not the live

"As far as we tinued, "it has b that three vess board, namely, pathia and the heard from C Olympic, that 1 minutes after le also learned fro had 675 surviv difficult to learn Parisian have We have asked agent at Halifa any passengers ships.

"We very mu has been a gre possible for us

Frien

Supreme C assure

Anxious inqu of the Interna were assured t yesterday that though ever two o'clock y been beneath t

All officials most confidence not offer any d the vessel, bu to be press dee dian points, fi from the master "the Parisian to the rescue of

Prisoners of friends and rel offices in the some were so away smiling Star line, which national Merca the usual aspe fate of a vesse cause all who convinced by th

registered 30.20 inches, indicating an absence of fog.

Many of the passengers aboard the giant steamship were men of world-wide prominence. Among these were Colonel and Mrs. John Jacob Astor, Bruce Ismay, W. T. Stead, the famous London journalist, who was on his way to New York to take part in the meeting this week of the Men and Religion Forward Movement; Mr. and Mrs. Isidor Straus, Clarence Moore, the Countess of Rothes, Major Archibald Butt, military secretary to President Taft; Benjamin Guggenheim, the head of vast commercial and financial interests; J. B. Thayer, vice president of the Pennsylvania Railroad; Colonel Washington Roebling, Colonel Archibald Gracie, Mr. and Mrs. Frederick R. Hoyle, F. D. Millet, the artist; Henry B. Harris, theatrical manager; Mr. and Mrs. J. B. Thayer, Mr. and Mrs. George B. Widener, Mr. J. Stuart White, Mrs and Mrs. Henry Harper, Charles M. Hays, president of the Grand Trunk Pacific, of Canada, and many others prominent in the commercial, professional or social life of this and other cities.

Should the present estimates of the fatalities be sustained no maritime disaster in the history of deep sea voyaging approaches in magnitude that of the loss of the Titanic.

The Atlantic went down, in 1873, with a loss of 574 lives. On the day when Sampson's ships destroyed the Spanish fleet at Santiago, La Bourgogne met her fate in collision with another vessel and her victims numbered 571.

These are the nearest approaches to the overwhelming casualty indicated by present advices. Should it prove that other ships, notably the Allan liners, the Parisian and the Virginian, which are known to have been in the vicinity of the Titanic yesterday morning, had rescued others of the passengers, the sweep-

List of Those Rescued Contains Names of Only Few Men

CAPE RACE, N. F., Monday.— Following is a list in part of the first-class passengers who were rescued from the Titanic:—
Mrs. Edward W. Appleton.
Mrs. Rose Abbott.
Mrs. G. M. Burns.
Miss D. D. Cassebere.
Mrs. William M. Clarke.
Mrs. B. Chibinace.
Miss E. G. Crossbie.
Miss H. E. Crosbie.
Miss Jean Hippach.
Mrs. Henry B. Harris(wireless version Mrs. L. Y. B. Harris).
Mrs. Alex Halverson.
Miss Margaret Hays.
Mr. J. Bruce Ismay.
Mr. and Mrs. Ed Kimberley.
Mr. F. A. Kenyman.
Miss Emile Kenchen.
Miss G. F. Longley.
Miss A. F. Leader.
Miss Bertha Lavery.

Mrs. Ernest Lives.
Mrs. Susan P. Rogerson.
Miss Emily B. Rogerson.
Mrs. Arthur Rogerson.
Master Allison and nurse, Miss K. T. Andrews.
Miss Ninette Panhart.
Miss E. W. Allen.
Mr. and Mrs. D. Bishop.
Mr. H. Blank.
Miss A. Bassina.
Mrs. James Baxter.
Mr. George A. Bayton.
Miss C. Bonnell.
Mrs. J. M. Brown.
Miss G. C. Bowen.
Mr. and Mrs. R. L. Beckwith.
The list was received by wireless at Cape Race station from the steamer Carpathia. In spellings and initials it does not correspond with the list as cabled from London to-day.
Mrs. F. M. Warner.

Miss Helen A. Wilson.
Miss Willard.
Miss Mary Wicks.
Mrs. George D. Widener and maid, Mrs. J. Stewart.
Miss Mary Clines.
Mrs. Singrid Lindstrom.
Mr. Gustav J. Lesneur.
Miss Georgietta Amadile.
Mme. Mellcard.
Mrs. Tucker and maid.
Mrs. J. B. Thayer.
Mr. J. B. Thayer, Jr.
Mr. H. Woolmer.
Miss Anna Ward.
Mr. Rich M. William.
Mrs. J. Steward White.
Miss Marie Young.
Mrs. Thomas Potter, Jr.
Mrs. Edna S. Roberts.
Countess of Rothes.
Mrs. C. Rolmane.
Mrs. Jacob P. (word missed).

NEW YORK HERALD, WEDNESDAY, APRIL 17, 1912.

HOPE, THRONGS AWAIT S

WHO ARE REPORTED MISSING.

SOME OF THE SURVIVORS OF T

GEORGE D. WIDENER.

GEORGE RHEIMS.
PHOTO BY DANA E. SANFORD.

QUES FUTRELLE

EMIL BRANDEIS.

BROTHERS RESCUED WITH THE DOCTOR'S BRIDE

DR. HENRY W. FRAUENTHAL.

COLONEL ARCHIBALD GRACIE.

KARL H. BEHR.

I. GERRY FRAUENTHAL.

SAVED FROM THE DISASTER.

D MRS A HARDER

Latest List of Survivors

This list of survivors of first class passengers was issued by P. A. S. Franklin, the vice president, at the office of the White Star line late last night. In making it public Mr. Franklin said that the list had been gone over and checked up by cable with the London office of the company. These survivors are among those known to be aboard the incoming Carpathia.

A

ANDERSON, HARRY.
APPLETON, Mrs. E. D., Bayside, L. I.
ABBOTT, Mrs. ROSE
ALLISON, Master, and nurse.
ANDREWS, Miss CORNELIA L., Newark, Ohio.
ALLEN, Miss ELIZABETH WALTON.
ASTOR, Mrs. JOHN JACOB, and maid.

B

BEHR, KARL H., No. 777 Madison avenue, city.
BESSETTE, Miss.
BUCKNELL, Mrs. WILLIAM
BARKWORTH, Mr. A. H.
BOWERMAN, Miss ELSIE.
BROWN, Mrs. J. M., Boston, Mass.
BURNS, Miss C. M.
BISHOP, Mr. and Mrs. D. H.
BLANK, HENRY.
BASSINA, Miss A.
BARRETT, KARL

K

KIMBALL, Mr. and Mrs. E. N.
KENNYMAN, Mr. F. A
KENCHEN, Miss EMILE.

L

LONGLEY, Miss GRETCHEN F., Newark, Ohio.
LEADER, Dr. ALICE F., No. 340 W. 118th street.
LAVORY, Miss BERTHA.
LINES, Mrs. ERNEST H.
LINES, Miss MARY C.
LINDSTROM, Mrs. SINGIRD.
LESNEUR, Mr. GUSTAVE, Jr.

M

MADILL, Miss GEORGETTE A., Louis, Mo.
MELICARD, Mme.
MIDDLE, OLIVIA.
MAIMY, Miss ROBERTA.
MARVIN, Mrs. D. W.
MARECHELL, Mr. PIERRE.
MINAHAN, Miss DAISY, Green B., Wis.
MINAHAN, Mrs., Fond-du-Lac, Wis.
NEWELL, Miss ALICE.
NEWELL, Mr. Washington.
NEWSOME, Miss HELEN, Columb, Ohio.

O

O'CONNELL, Miss R. (may be Mrs. Robert Cornell).

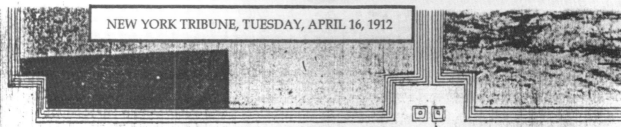
CAPTAIN E. J. SMITH ON THE BRIDGE OF THE TITANIC.
Although wireless reports are silent, it is believed he went down with his ship.

THE TITANIC, THE GREATE
FOUNDERED ON HER I

NAMES OF SURVIVORS ON THE CARPATHIA

Wireless Brings Partial List of First Cabin Passengers Saved from Titanic.

Cape Race, N. F., April 15.—Following is a partial list of the first cabin passengers who were rescued from the Titanic:

Mrs. Jacob P. —— (word missed),
Mrs. Edward W. Appleton.
Mrs. Rose Abbott.
Miss G. M. Burns.
Miss D. D. Cassebere.
Mrs. William M. Clarke.
Mrs. B. Chibinaco.
Miss E. G. Crossbie.
Miss H. E. Crossbie.
Miss Jean Hippach.
Mrs. Henry B. Harris (wireless version Mrs. L. Y. B. Harris).
Mrs. Alexander Halverson.
Miss Margaret Hays.
Mr. and Mrs. J. Bruce Ismay.
Mr. and Mrs. Ed Kimberley (according to wireless).
F. A. Kenyman.
Miss Emile Kenchen.
Miss G. F. Longley.
Miss A. F. Leader.
Miss Bertha Lavory.
Mrs. Ernest Lives.
Mrs. Susan P. Rogerson.
Miss Emily B. Rogerson.
Mrs. Arthur Rogerson.
Master Allison and nurse, Miss K. T. Andrews.
Miss Ninette Panhart.
Miss E. W. Allen.
Mr. and Mrs. T. D. Bishop.
H. Blank.
Miss A. Bassina.
Mrs. James Baxter.
George A. Bayton.
Miss C. Bonnell.
Mrs. J. M. Brown.
Miss G. C. Bowen.
Mr. and Mrs. R. L. Beckwith.
Mrs. F. M. Warner.
Miss Helen A. Wilson.
Miss Willard.
Miss Mary Wicks.
Mrs. George D. Widener and maid.
Miss Mary Clines.
Mrs. Singrid Lindstrom.
Gustav J. Lesneur.
Miss Georgietta Amadiii.
Mme. Mellcard.
Mrs. Tucker and maid.
Mrs. J. B. Thayer.
J. B. Thayer, Jr.
H. Woolmer.
Miss Anna Ward.
Richard M. William.
Mrs. J. Steward White.
Miss Marie Young.
Mrs. Thomas Potter, jr.
Mrs. Edna S. Roberts.
Mr. and Mrs. L. Henry.
Mrs. W. A. Hooper.
Mr. Mile.

J. Flynn.
Miss Alice Fortune.
Mrs. Robert Douglas.
Miss Hilda Slayter.
Mrs. P. Smith.
Mrs. Braham.
Miss Lucille Carter.
William Carter.
Miss Roberts.
Miss Cummings.
Countess of Rothes.
C. Rolmane.
Mrs. Florence Mare.
Miss Alice Phillips.
Mrs. Paula Munge.
Miss Rosie —— (word missed).
Mrs. Jane —— (word missed),
Miss Phyllis O. —— (word missed).
Miss Bertha —— (word missed).
Mrs. Carl H. Behr.
Miss Bessette.
Mrs. William Bucknell.
A. H. Beekworth.
H. B. Steffason.
Mrs. Elsie E. Bowerman.
Mrs. D. W. Marvin.
Philip Emock.
James Googht.
Miss Ruberta Maimy.
Pierre Marechal.
Mrs. W. E. Minahan.
Miss Minahan.
Miss Appie Ranelt.
Major Arthur Peuchen.
Miss Ruth Taussig.
Miss Ella Thor.
Mr. and Mrs. E. Z. Taylor.
Gilbert M. Tucker.
J. B. Thayer.
John Rogerson (probably Ryerson).
Mrs. M. Rothschild.
Miss Madeleine Newell.
Mrs. Marjorie Newell.
Mrs. Helen W. Newson.
Flennal Omond.
E. C. Ostby.
Miss Helen R. Ostby.
Mrs. Maman J. Renago.
Middle Olivia.

The above list was received by wireless at Cape Race station from the steamer Carpathia. In spelling and initials it does not correspond with the list as cabled from London to-day.

One of the most serious errors in the wireless list of survivors appears to be in giving four members of the "Rogerson" family. No such name appears in

Continued on second page, fifth column.

"LOSS 1,800 OLYM

Belief Here That I Large by 300---F

The text of the message sinking of the Titanic and the here late last night, also expres

"Loss likely total 1,800 so sentence.

It is hoped and believed Titanic had more passengers about 2,200 persons, includin, the known saved, would indica

The Olympic's dispatch for

"Carpathia reached Titan wreckage only. Titanic sank All her boats accounted for, ed passengers included. Nearly liner Californian remained a Loss likely total 1,800 souls."

TITANIC TWO MILES D

This the Depth of Ocean W the Liner Went Down.

Halifax, April 15.—The deathb the $10,000,000 steamer Titanic, probably many who must have dragged down with her, is two mi least, below the surface of the sea

This calculation was made by a cial of the government Marine D ment, who finds that depth on th rine chart at a point about five h miles from Halifax and about s miles south of the Grand Banks, he believes the Titanic went down

This location is midway between Island and Cape Race, and in line those dangerous sands which, ho might have proved a place of safe there been time to run the Titanic and beach her.

First Cabin Passengers Known To Be Saved

Franklin Gives List Checked Up by Cable with London Office.

The following list of survivors of first class passengers was issued by Vice-President Franklin at the office of the White Star Line at 3:45 p. m. yesterday afternoon. In making it public Mr. Franklin said that the list had been gone over and checked up by cable with the London office of the company. The survivors named are among those known to be aboard the incoming Cunarder Carpathia:

A

Anderson, Harry.
Appleton, Mrs. E. W.
Abbott, Mrs. Rose.
Allison, Master, and nurse.
Andrews, Miss K. T. (Miss Cornelia?)
Allen, Miss E. W.
Astor, Mrs. John Jacob, and maid.

B

Barratt, Karl B. (Behr?)
Bessette, Miss.
Bucknell, Mrs. William.
Barthworth, A. H. (Bathworth?)
Bowerman, Miss E.
Brown, Mrs. J. J.
Burns, Miss C. M.
Bishop, Mr. and Mrs. D.
Blank, H.
Bessina, Miss A.
Baxter, Mrs. James.
Bayton, George A.
Bonnell, Miss C.
Brown, Mrs. J. M.
Bowen, Miss G. C.
Beckwith, Mr. and Mrs. R. L.

C

Cassebere, Miss D. D.
Clarke, Mrs. W. M.
Chibinaco, Mrs. B.
Crossbie, Miss E. G.
Carter, Miss Lucille.
Carter, Mrs. William.
Cander, Mrs. Churchill (Cardell?)
Calderhead, N. P.
Chandanson, Miss Victorine.
Cavendish, Mrs. Turrell, and maid.
Chaffee, Mrs. H. L.
Cardeza, Mr. and Mrs. Thomas.
Cummings, Mrs. J.
Chiver, Paul (Chèvre?)
Cherry, Miss Gladys.
Chambers, Mr. and Mrs. B. C.
Carter, Mr. and Mrs. W. E.
Carter, Master William.

D

Douglass, Mrs. Fred.
De Villien, Mme. (Mrs. B. de Villiers?)
Daniel, Robert W.
Davidson, Mr. and Mrs. Thornton, and family.
Douglas, Mrs. Walter.
Dodge, Miss Sarah.
Dodge, Mrs. Washington, and son.
Dick, Mr. and Mrs.
Daniell, H. Haren.
Drachenstad, A.

E

Emmock, Philip E.
Endres, Miss Caroline.
Ellis, Miss.
Earnshaw, Miss Boulton (Mrs.?)

F

Flegenheim, Miss Antoinette.
Francatelli, Miss.
Flynn, J. N. (J. I.?)
Fortune, Miss Alice.
Fortune, Miss.
Fortune, Mrs. Mark.
Fortune, Miss Mabel.
Frauenthal, Mr. and Mrs. Hy. W. (Dr.?)
Frauenthal, Mr. and Mrs. J. G. (T. G.?)
Frolicher, Miss Margaret.
Futrelle, Mrs. Jacques.

G

Gracie, Colonel Arthur (Archibald?)

Graham, Mr. and Mrs. William.
Graham, Miss.
Gordon, Sir Cosmo Duff.
Gordon, Lady.
Gibson, Miss Dorothy.
Gildenberg, Mrs. Samuel.
Goldenberg, Miss Ella.
Greenfield, William (G. B.?)
Greenfield, William.
Gibson, Mrs. Leonard.
Googht, James.

H

Harris, L. Y. B. (Mrs.?)
Halverson, Mrs. Alex.
Hogiboom, Mrs. I. C.
Hawksford, W. J.
Harper, Henry, and man servant.
Harper, Mrs. H. S.
Hoyt, Mr. and Mrs. Fred.
Horner, Hy. R. (Homer?)
Harder, Mr. and Mrs. George.
Hays, Mrs. Charles M., and daughter.
Hippach, Miss Jean.
Hippach, Mrs. Ida S.

I

Ismay, J. Bruce.

K

Kimberley, Mr. and Mrs. Ed. (L. N. Kimball?)
Kennyman, F. A.
Kenchen, Miss Emile.

L

Longley, Miss G. F.
Leader, Mrs. A. F.
Lavory, Miss Bertha.
Lines, Mrs. Ernest.
Lines, Miss Mary.
Lindstrom, Mrs. Singird.
Lesneur, Gustave, jr.

M

Madill, Miss Georgette A.
Melicard, Mme.
Maimy, Miss Roberta.
Marvin, Mrs. D. W. (Martin?)
Marechell, Pierre.
Minehan, Mrs. Daisy (Minanhan?)
Minahan, Mrs. (Minanhan?)

N

Newell, Mrs. Marjorie (Miss Alice?)
Newell, Mrs. Madeline (Miss?)
Newell, Washington.
Newson, Miss Helen.

O

O'Connell, Miss R.
Ostby, Mr. and Mrs.
Ostby, Miss Helen.
Olivia, Miss.
Omond, Miss Anam.

P

Panhart, Miss Ninette.
Potter, Mrs. Thomas, jr. (Porter?)
Pincham, Major Arthur (Penchen?)

R

Rogerson, John.
Renago, Mrs. Mamam.
Ranelt, Miss Appie.
Rothchild, Mrs. Lord Martin.

Continued on fourth page, fifth column.

LATEST CORRECTED LIST OF THE TITANIC'S SURVIVORS

CAPE RACE, Newfoundland, April 17.—The steamship Carpathia, which is believed to have on board all the survivors of the Titanic disaster, yesterday sent by wireless to this station the list of those saved. Great difficulty was experienced in getting many of the names correctly, and more than a score of names as made out here did not appear at all on the Titanic's original passenger list, but it is believed that many of these were passengers who had booked at the last moment. More than six hours' effort was required for the receipt of the list of the first-cabin survivors.

So far as the names check up correctly, the following saloon passengers of the Titanic are safe on board the Carpathia as far as was known at 3 o'clock this afternoon:

ANDERSON, Harry.
ALLEN, Miss E. W.
APPLETON, Mrs. E. W.
ASTOR, Mrs. John Jacob and maid.
BARKWORTH, A. H.
BARRETT, Karl.
BAXTER, Mrs. James.
BRAYTON, George A.
BECKWITH, Mr. and Mrs. R. T.
BEHR, Karl H.
BESSETTE, Miss.
BISHOP, Mr. and Mrs. D. H.
BLANK, Henry.
BONNELL, Miss Caroline.
BOWEN, Miss G. C.
BOWERMAN, Miss Elsie.
BROWN, Mrs. J. M.
BROWN, Mrs. J. J.
CALDERHEAD, E. P.
CARDELL, Mrs. Churchill.
CARDEZA, Mrs. J. W.
CARDEZA, Thomas.
CARTER, Miss Lucille.
CARTER, Mr. W. E.
CARTER, Mrs. William E.
CARTER, Master William.
CASE, Howard B.
CAVENDISH, Mrs. Turrell W., and maid.
CHAFFEE, Mrs. H. F.
CHAMBERS, Mr. and Mrs. N. C.
CHAMDASEN, Mrs. Victorine.
CHERRY, Miss Gladys.
CHEVRO, Paul.
CLARKE, Mrs. Walter.
CROSBY, Mrs. E. G.
CROSBY, Miss.
CUMMINGS, Mrs. John B.
DANIEL, Robert W.
DANIEL, Miss Sarah.
DAVIDSON, Mrs. Thornton.
DESETTE, Miss.
DEVELLIERS, Mrs. B.
DICK, Mr. and Mrs. A. A.
DODGE, Mr. and Mrs. Washington and son.
DOUGLAS, Mrs. Fred C.
DOUGLAS, Mrs. Walter.
DRAUCHENSTED, Alfred.
EMOCK, Philip.
ENDRES, Mrs. Caroline.
FARNSHAW, Mrs. Bolton.
FLEGHEIM, Miss Antoinette.
FLYNN, J. F.
FORTUNE, Mrs. Mark, Miss Lucille, Miss Alice.
FRANSATELLI, Miss.
FRAUENTHAL, Dr. Henry and Mrs.
FRAUENTHAL, Mr. and Mrs. T. G.
FROLICHER, Miss Margaret.
FUTRELLE, Mrs. Jacques.
GIBSON, Mrs. Leonard.
GIBSON, Miss Dorothy.

NEWSOM, Miss Helen.
OSTBY, R. C.
OSTBY, Mrs.
OSTBY, Miss Helen R.
OMOND, Mr. Flennad.
PANHART, Miss Nannette.
PEUCHEN, Maj. Arthur.
POTTER, Mrs. Thomas, jr.
RANELT, Miss Apple.
REMAGO, Mrs. Hamman J.
RHEIMS, Mrs. George.
ROBERT, Mrs. Edward S.
ROLMANO, C.
ROSENBAUM, Miss Edith.
ROTHSCHILD, Mrs. Martin.
ROTHES, Countess of.
SAALFELD, Adolphe.
SALAMAN, Abraham.
SCHABERT, Mrs. Paul.
SEGESSER, Miss Emma.
SEREPECA, Miss Augusta.
SEWARD, Frederick.
SHADELI, Robert Douglas.
SILVERTHORNE, R. Spencer.
SILVEY, Mrs. William D.
SIMONIUS, Col. Alfonso.
SLAYTON, Miss Hilda.
SLOPER, William T.
SMITH, Mrs. Lucien P.
SMITH, Mrs. P. P.
STEFFANSON, H. B.
STEPHENSON, Mrs. P.
THAYER, Mr. and Mrs. J. B.
THOR, Miss Ella.
TUCKER, Mrs. and maid.
WARD, Miss Emma.
WILLARD, Miss Constance.
WOOLNER, Hugh.
YOUNG, Miss Marie.

Other First Cabin Survivors.

NEW YORK, April 16.—The following list of first-class survivors is additional to the list under a Cape Race date:

DODGE, Miss Sarah.
DANIEL, Mr. H. Haren.
FANTINI, Mrs. Mark.
HAYS, Miss Margaret.
NEWELL, Mrs. Washington.
ROSIBER, Miss H.
STEPHENSON, Mrs. Walter.
WILSON, Miss Helen A.

Some Question as to Identity.

In the following list the names as received by wireless are given their probable interpretation.

ABBOTT, Mrs. ROSE (probably Mrs. N. Auburt).
ANDREWS, Miss K. T. (probably Miss CORNELIA I).
CHIBINACE, Mrs. B. (probably Mrs. E. B. CHIBNALL).
DOUGLAS, ROBERT (probably Mr. or Mrs. W. DOUGLASS, or Mrs. F. C. CORNELIA I).
ELLIS, Miss (may be Miss EUSTIA).
KENCHEN, Miss EMILE (possibly Mrs. F. R. KENYON.
KIMBERLEY, Mr. and Mrs. ED (possibly Mr. and Mrs. E. N. KIMBALL).
KENNYMAN, F. A. (probably Mr. or Mrs. F. R. Kenyon).
LINDSTROM, SINGRID (probably Mrs. J. LINDSTROM).
MILE (probably FRANK D. MILLET).
ROGERSON, Mr. J., Mrs. ARTHUR, Miss EMILY B., Miss SUSAN P., Master ALLISON, and maid (practically certain this is RYERSON family of Philadelphia).
SHUTTER, Miss (probably Miss E. W. SCHUTES).
SPEDDEN, Mr. and Mrs. J. J. (probably Mr. and Mrs. FREDERICK O. SPEDDEN).
WILLIAMS, RICH N. (probably N. M. WILLIAMS, jr.)
O'CONNELL, Mrs. Robert (probably Mrs. R. C. CORNELL).

Not on the Sailing List.

The following is a list of survivors whose names do not appear on the original sailing list, and probably included a large number of those who took the ship at Cherbourg:

BASSINA, Miss A.
BARRATT, KARL.
BESSETTE, Miss.
BUCKNELL, Mrs. WILLIAM.
BURNS, Mrs. G. M.
CASEBERE, Miss D. D.
HASSIG, MILE.

DAVIS, John M.
DURAN, Florentina.
DURAN, Ascuncion.
DAVIS, Miss Mary.
DOLING, Mrs. Ada.
DOLING, Miss Elsie.
FAUNTHROPE, Mrs. Lizzie.
GARSIDE, Miss Ethel.
HAMALANIAN, W.
HAMALANIAN, H.
HEWLETT, Miss Mary D.
HARRIS, George.
HERMAN, Mrs. Jane.
HERMAN, Miss Kate.
HERMAN, Miss Alice.
HOLD, Miss Annie.
HART, Mrs. Esther.
HART, Miss Eva.
HARPER, Miss Nina.
HAMALINER, Anna and son.
HOCKING, Mrs. Elizabeth.
HOCKING, Miss Nellie.
JACOBSOHN, Mrs. Amy.
KEANE, Miss Nora.
KELLY, Miss Fannie.
LAROCHE, Miss Louisa.
LEITCH, Miss Jessie W.
LAMORE, Mrs.
LOUCH, Mrs. Alice.
LEHMAN, Miss Bertha.
MELLINGER, Mrs. Elizabeth and child.
MALLET, Mrs. A.
MALLET, Master Adrero.
NYE, Mrs. Elizabeth.
PHILLIPS, Miss Alice.
PAILAS, Emilio.
PADRO, Julian.
PARISH, Mrs. L.
PORTALUPPI, Mrs. Emilio.
QUICK, Mrs. Jane O.
QUICK, Miss Wennie O.
QUICK, Miss Phyllis O.
REBOUF, Mrs. Lillie.
RIDSDALE, Mrs. Lucy.
RUGG, Miss Emily.
RICHARD, Mr. and Mrs. Emile and son.
HINCOCK, Miss Maude.
SMITH, Mrs. Marion.
TROUT, Miss Edna S.
WEISZ, Mrs. Matilda.
WEBBER, Miss Susan.
WRIGHT, Miss Marion.
WATT, Miss Bessie.
WATT, Miss Bertha.
WEST, Mrs. and two children.
WELLS, Mrs. Addie.
WELLS, Miss J.
WELLS, Ralph.
WILLIAMS, Charles.

Question as to Identity.

Following is a list of second-cabin survivors about whose identity there is some question, there being a discrepancy between the wireless version and the names on the booking list:

BECKER, Mrs. Allen; Miss Ruth, Miss Mary, Master Richard; undoubtedly the same as given in sailing list under names of "Mrs. A. O. Beiker and three children."
JULIET, Mr. Laroche; Mr. Laroche Simone; probably Mrs. Joseph Laroche and Simon Laroche.
LINKKANCA, Miss Anna; probably Mrs. William Lahtigen.
MARSHALL, Miss Kate; probably Mrs. Marshall.
MANGE, Mr. Paula; may be Mrs. William Angle.
MALLCROFT, Miss Millie; probably Miss Nellie Walcroft.
MELLORS, J. N.; may be William Mellors.
NASERAELL, Mrs. Adella; probably Mrs. Nicholas Nassar.
OXENHAM, Percy J.; may be Thomas Oxenham.
ROGERS, Miss Eliza; may be Selina Rogers.
SILWANA, Miss Synly; may be Lillie Silven.

Not on Sailing List.

Following is a list of survivors whose names do not appear on the original sailing list:

8d

A False Identity ?

On Thursday, 18th April the *Carpathia* docked at New York. Possibly one of the weariest of the *Titanic's* survivors to disembark was the young Marconi operator, Harold Bride. Having worked to the last on board the *Titanic,* sending out messages to any vessel near enough to come to her aid, after a few hours respite aboard the *Carpathia* he was again back at work. Here he assisted the ship's own operator in sending out the information from which the newspapers printed lists of the lost or saved.

Was it he or his colleague who became the unwitting instrument used to lay yet another ridiculous charge against my mother, Nurse Cleaver ? Was it he who inadvertently enabled a comma to creep in where a full stop should have taken its place ?

You may feel this to be unimportant and I would be the first to agree, were it not that an innocent and seemingly insignificant error has allowed a less innocent conclusion to be reached.

In relating the arrival of the *Carpathia* at New York, and the survivors encountering the waiting press, Mr Lynch tells us -

"As the reporters mobbed around, Alice fended them off with fresh falsehoods, giving her first name as "Jane" and refusing to provide a surname. In a bizarre twist, the press simply assumed that "Jane" was in fact the "Miss K.T. Andrews" whose name followed that of "Master Allison and nurse" on the list of survivors. The public, eager for heroes, did not question Alice's story of selfless sacrifice, and her true identity remained unknown."

This is pure unadulterated nonsense. My mother would not have given her name as *"Jane"*, for *"Jane"* was not her name. I have scoured as many newspapers as possible for reports of these *"fresh falsehoods"*, and failed to find any. I cannot say for certain that some obscure and inaccurate reference does not exist - it is very difficult to prove a negative, but how easy to prove a positive. If somewhere a mention does occur then what could be the harm in the author naming his source ? Or are we supposed to believe him misled by some ancient newspaper man, who remembers my mother stating her name to be *"Jane"*, but never thought it sufficiently significant at the time to add it to his printed report ? No, his refusal to name a source, along with the lack of any reason for her to have *"fended them off with fresh falsehoods"*, leaves me in little doubt as to the truth.

If the reference to *"Jane"* is strange then how much stranger is the supposed connection of *"Jane"* with *"Miss K.T. Andrews"*, by the press, when the two are such widely differing names ?

However, Mr Lynch does give us a glimpse of the truth when he refers back to *"on the list of survivors."*

I have already touched on the small matter of a comma, and as can be seen in the reproduced extracts from the newspapers (fronting this chapter), its importance has grown out of all proportion to its size. For, whereas from the first lists of the 16th, the *New York Times* knew and showed *"Master ALLISON and nurse"* to be a separate party to Miss Andrews, some of the other papers were deceived by a comma following *nurse*. Instead of taking Miss Andrews as the next passenger on the list, they took this to be the nurse's name. The *New York Times* was not alone in its correct presentation, other papers that failed to confuse the identities of the two included *The World*, New York and the *New York Evening Post*, and British papers from the evening of the 16th - *Southern Daily Echo* (Southampton) and the *Liverpool Echo*. British nationals such as *The Times, The Daily Telegraph* and the *Daily Mirror*, first printed lists of survivors the following morning, the 17th, at which time all were correct in their appraisal.

The papers which at first reported the Allison nurse as being Miss Andrews included the *New York Tribune, New York Herald* and *Chicago Daily Tribune*. By the 17th, newspapers had corrected their survivors' lists, differentiating between the nurse and Miss Andrews, as illustrated by extracts of that date from both the above New York papers. The *Chicago Daily Tribune*, however, removed mention of Master Allison (and his nurse) from its lists of the saved. But now they, and the maid, were included with his parents and sister as *"feared drowned"*.

The Canadian papers did not on the whole go in for lists in the same way as the American press, and were much less comprehensive, tending in the main to print names of more localised interest. Once done they did not continually return to update them.

In the case of the *Toronto Globe*, my mother appears along with her charge on the 16th as - *"Master Allison, and nurse, Miss K.T. Andrews"*, but on the very next day under *"CANADIANS LOST"* appears *"Mrs. Allison and son, Montreal"*. The Allison daughter who was actually lost, not her baby brother, is shown under *"CANADIANS SAVED"*. On the 19th, the front page continues to refer to *"the baby Allison and her* [sic] *nurse"*, despite an article a few pages later mentioning the survivor as a *"baby boy"*. The *Toronto Evening Telegram* was likewise confused as to the fate of the Allisons. Their edition of the 16th noted Mrs Allison and her daughter as saved, but by the next day *both* Allison children were described as victims.

The extract from the *Washington Evening Star* underlines the confusion. Under *"Some Question as to Identity"* on 17th

April, *"Master ALLISON, and maid"* were included in with the Rogersons as *"(practically certain this is RYERSON family of Philadelphia)"*, when of course the Allisons were unconnected, and instead of maid it should have said nursemaid.

~~~~~

I have disputed my mother giving her name as *"Jane"*, for she would not have given a false name, simply had no reason to do so and there is no evidence to that effect. I further dispute the suggestion that the confusion with Miss Andrews took place on their arrival in New York. The newspapers are clear evidence that it *occurred* days before the *Carpathia* docked, and was *corrected* days before she docked. I would have been most surprised to find that the press at New York, on speaking to the young English nurse, would have mistaken her for Miss Andrews, a native New Yorker in her sixties. The latter would, at the date in question, have been considered an elderly woman. Miss Andrews was accompanied by her sister and a niece, how could they bear any similarity to the survivors of the Allison party ?

Admittedly, at a later date some newspapers did refer to the nurse once again as Miss Andrews, when for instance showing photographs. They seemed to have the habit, even many years later, when harking back to an old story, of repeating initial errors and ignoring their subsequent corrected version.

To seek to apportion blame to the individuals named, for errors concerning them in the survivors' lists, is grossly unfair. Just the few brief extracts reproduced here confirm the doubts raised by the newspapers over some identities. They are littered with *"probably"*, *"may be"*, *"word missing"* and questioned names. Anyone who has spent even a minimal amount of time studying the papers, will be only too aware of the many inaccuracies and inconsistencies contained within them. I have come across a number whilst engaged purely on research in relation to my mother, and no doubt there are very many more examples to be had.

For instance, if we look at the Allison party alone, then Mr Allison himself was on occasion identified as being an American senator, and shown as a white-haired, bearded man, at least twice as old as the young Canadian banker he actually was.

Mrs Allison's maid was frequently recorded as lost along with her mistress, i.e. as Mrs Allison and maid. The papers, never really appreciating the maid's identity, also showed her independently under her own name, Sarah Daniels, in the lists of the saved. The *New York Tribune* as late as the 21st (three days after the survivors had arrived in the city), states under the list of women and children who perished - *"Allison, Mrs., and maid"*.

Certain survivors' lists included a Sarah Dodge. The Dodge family, if they knew, would have been most surprised to find an addition to their number. There is some evidence for this too being the Allison maid. Although a few papers did give both names at the same time (e.g. *New York Evening Post*, 17th), in others the entries for Sarah Dodge disappeared only to be replaced by Sarah Daniels (e.g. *The World*, New York, 19th April). With both of these names, it was often noted that they did not appear on the original passenger lists. The maid, like the other servants, would have been shown on those only as an appendant to her mistress.

~~~~~

Leaving the Allison family to one side, survivor Lawrence Beesley had good reason to feel concern about the inaccuracy of these lists. In his book, *The Loss of the S.S. Titanic*, Mr Beesley went into some detail on this subject, and the official roll-call of the rescued held on board the *Carpathia*. He describes how his marconigram never reached his friends, despite the roll-call his name failed to appear in the lists of the saved, and refers to how *"even a week after landing in New York, I saw it in a black-edged "final" list of the missing"*. It must have been a rather strange experience for the young Dulwich Schoolmaster, on disembarking at New York, to find himself considered dead, and to be in the position of reading his own obituary in the English press.

Far more tragic is the account he gives, wherein the son of a stated survivor discovered only at New York that the inaccuracy of these lists had not prepared the family for the cruel truth. His father had, contrary to reports, perished in the disaster, never in fact reaching the *Carpathia.*

Mr Lynch would have us believe that my mother was in some way responsible for the inaccurate information printed about herself, that she was trying to conceal her *"true identity"*. Does he suggest Mr Beesley faked his own death, or that the unfortunate man described, who did not survive, was the engineer of his family's false hopes ? I think not.

Returning briefly to Mr Beesley. If a thoroughly absorbing yet sensible account from a passenger's point of view, someone truly in a position to provide this, is wanted, then it seems to me he was admirably suited to the task. My only reservation - I'm afraid it is too sensible for some. For Lawrence Beesley was intent on capturing the accurate atmosphere aboard both the *Titanic* and *Carpathia*, dismissing the sensationalist elements and myths, which even then had begun to grow out of the disaster.

Subsequent authors have also highlighted the reliability or otherwise of the reporting. Walter Lord referring in *A Night to Remember* to *"most of the New York papers"* with the exception of the *Times*, as being *"extremely unreliable."* Michael Davie, himself a reporter, in his book, *The Titanic: The Full Story of a Tragedy,* writes of the difficulties and demands placed on the newspapers, particularly in relation to the arrival of the survivors at New York. Also recognising that there was another side to this - *"less scrupulous reporters knew that what they wrote could never be checked. Friday* [19th] *morning's papers thus released a flood of unreliable information on the world."* He then details some of the outlandish stories that went to print.

This unreliability may appear more obvious when commenting on the overdramatic stories of scenes on board the *Titanic,* but there is little doubt that it was just as present in the lists of those lost and saved.

Mr Lynch has been researching and analysing these *Titanic* sources for over twenty years. His familiarity with them is not in question. Consequently, for him to pick on any of these inaccuracies, to wrongly attribute their origin (which has clearly been shown to predate the one he states) and use to single out an individual survivor as a liar is extremely misleading. Moreover, his parting shot *"her true identity remained unknown"* is untrue. My mother was known as Master Allison's nurse, as was correct in the context of the times, just as other servants were similarly described by their employers' names and not their own. If some members of the press were daft enough to assign another person's name to her, was that her fault ?

As to Nurse Cleaver's *"story of selfless sacrifice"*, here I have failed miserably in my quest, for it seems although the public of the day were so aware of this, the therefore widespread coverage it must have achieved has passed me by. It is a shame that Mr Lynch does not point out where this appears because, as her daughter, I would be most interested in seeing what I know to be the truth, so far I have only seen my mother's bravery referred to.

8e

Appearances can be Deceptive

To study what I consider to be the least serious but most uncharitable of charges against my mother, Nurse Cleaver, it is apt to return to the *good old days*, before we were corrupted by Hollywood of the talkies. But are we not so much more sophisticated now, that we no longer need the writer or director to tell us which character is good and which evil by presenting us with the appropriate stereotype, as in the days of the old silent movies ?

Yet, to my mind, this is exactly what Mr Lynch does when including a picture from the *Chesterville Record,* accompanied with this, *his* caption -

"Although most newspapers retouched Alice Cleaver's face to make the supposed heroine look more pleasant, the Chesterville (Ontario) Record showed her as she actually appeared."

Now we are left in no doubt, here is the villain of the piece - evil personified, her unpleasant countenance revealing her true colours. So it seems the charge is that of being of an unprepossessing appearance. This is a charge from which I am reluctant to defend my mother. Although it has been set up as yet another

thing that should count against her, to my way of thinking someone's personal appearance is not generally a reflection of their
character as he implies.

Whilst an extremely pleasant visage may be accompanied
by an equally pleasant nature, it is not necessarily so, and the same
is true of a less attractive outward appearance. In some societies
the pursuit of beauty may be paramount, but if you take this
argument to its logical conclusion, do all those who successfully
enhance their looks also improve their inner qualities ?

Does beauty show inner goodness, ugliness inner evil and
plainness something in between ? What then of disfigurement,
disability and illness, which all affect our appearance ? It seems
that a *"supposed heroine"* is meant to look attractive, if you do
not meet with these standards then doing anything heroic is
apparently a waste of time, because it is not your actions that
count, but your looks.

This is by no means to acknowledge my mother as someone who looked unattractive or even unpleasant, but that it is
completely irrelevant whether she did or not. What is relevant are
the facts, something I at least intend to introduce into this subject:-

Firstly, this critic of my mother makes reference to how she
"actually appeared." How does he know this ? He never met her
then, or since. His opinion is formed merely on an old newspaper
photograph. All but the most conceited of us have derived
embarrassment and merriment in equal measure, when viewing
certain photographs of ourselves. Whether it be school, passport,
family snapshot or other photographs would you in fairness
wish to be judged on some of these which often seem intent in
capturing the least resemblance to those they claim to represent ?

Secondly, we are not discussing pictures taken on a joyful
occasion, but shortly after a disaster in which over 1,500 people
lost their lives. Many survivors have referred to the screams of the
dying, emanating from the *Titanic,* and noted how these would be
remembered as long as they lived. In the aftermath of this, some
may have looked cheerful and happy, my mother would not and
none of us look our best when we are feeling miserable, let alone

if we had been involved in such a tragedy. Think back to some particularly low points in your life and then imagine yourself in a strange land, subjected to the flashlights of a hungry press.

Thirdly, the photograph itself cannot be said to be of excellent quality, and without doubt is not a good photograph of my mother. Whether this was taken outside in natural daylight, or more likely indoors (in view of the time of year), the strong light is unmistakable by the contrasting shadows and white background. The critic's cut-down version shows the subject's frown while conveniently not showing the reason for it.

Quite frankly, I feel that Mr Lynch, as a representative of a *Titanic* society, ought to be thoroughly ashamed of himself for seeing fit to judge and make such a personal attack on the appearance of a young woman survivor, who had just gone through a very traumatic experience.

His public criticism of my mother, Nurse Cleaver's appearance, his judgement and stated opinion on her in this, as in every other matter, is more a reflection on him. Those in whom he expresses equal interest, the officers and gentlemen on board the *Titanic*, would have given short shrift to such an ungallant attack on a children's nursemaid by a man in his position.

So far I have discussed the merits of judgement of appearance, based on photographs taken under such circumstances and in such a way, but what of the statement itself ? How accurate is this ? Well, to start with much is pure conjecture, unless Mr Lynch was present at the various newspaper offices at the time, how can he claim that any *"retouched"* her face, let alone then enlarging on this with his reason why ?

I feel it is not an unfair inference to take from his caption, and particularly from the *"most newspapers"*, the idea that a reasonable number of other newspapers showed a similar (if not the same) photograph, but that the majority *"retouched"* prior to printing. Or that set alongside his text containing not only repeated references to survivors as they disembarked from the *Carpathia*, but also to the press awaiting them, that this photograph was taken in New York. This, however, is too simplistic and extremely misleading. As far as I have been able to establish, quite another photograph was taken in New York. This by Paul Thompson, and reproduced in the *New York Herald* on 24th April, printed also by the *Toronto Mail & Empire*, on the 26th, being attributed by them back to New York.

On Sunday, 28th April, both the *New York Times* and the *Washington Star*, included special sections on the *Titanic*. The similarity in text, and various pictures chosen, lead me to conclude that these special sections had an originator in common. Certainly both showed exactly the same picture of the Allison nurse, a stylized version of Paul Thompson's original photograph, acknowledging him as the source and repeating the error in caption - i.e. Nurse Andrews. Although these newspapers had previously avoided this error in their survivors' lists, now, a week after the Allison party had left New York, they picked it up with the photograph.

The picture, which Mr Lynch would like us to believe is the untouched version amongst the *"retouched"*, is quite a different picture from the one so far described above. Even the angle at which the nurse and baby are facing is different. This, as far as I can ascertain, was taken in Montreal on arrival there of the Allison party, and a few days later (on the 25th) appeared in the *Chesterville Record*, a weekly paper. But they were not alone in printing it, for it had already been shown in the *Montreal Daily Witness* of the 22nd, which may well have been the originating paper, and like the other pictures was probably published in other papers too.

So, all in all, we have different pictures, taken at different locations and therefore different times. This begs the question, where are the *"retouched"* photographs ? Instead Mr Lynch has chosen the worst picture he could find, setting aside the better ones of which he himself states he is aware.

Montreal Daily Witness, 22 April 1912 (top)
New York Herald, 24 April 1912 (middle)
New York Times, 28 April 1912 (bottom)

Youngest Survivor of the Titanic Gleeful with Foster Parents

BABY ALLISON AND NURSE ANDREWS OF MONTREAL WHO WERE SAVED FROM THE TITANIC WRECK.—THE BABY IS THE ONLY SURVIVOR OF THE ALLISON FAMILY

Boy, Eleven Months Old, Saved When Parents Went Down with Wreck, Becomes Centre of Much Attention and Smiles Happily.

Although Travers J. Allison, eleven months old, did not realize it yesterday, much interest was centred in his case. He is probably the most youthful survivor of the Titanic disaster. One would never think he had undergone such an experience to see him smiling and chuckling under the care of foster-parents at the Manhattan Hotel. He is the son of Mr. and Mrs. Hudson J. Allison, of Montreal. Mr. Hudson was a capitalist in that city and had various interests. When the Titanic went down the Allisons were on board, with two other children, a chauffeur and a maid.

During the rush and panic when lifeboats were lowered the Allison baby was found on the deck and taken aboard the next to the last lifeboat that went over the sides. It is doubtful if another person in the wrecked party received more care and attention than he. He did not seem to be any worse for his experience yesterday and smiled heartily when his picture was taken.

BRAVE NURSE AND THE BABE SHE SAVED

Nurse Cleaver, and the little baby Allison, whom she saved from the wreck, in which Mr. and Mrs. Allison and their little daughter were drowned.

Baby Allison and Miss Andrews, a Nurse, Titanic Survivors. The Baby Was the Only Survivor of the Allison Family, Passengers on the Sunken Liner.

Returning once again to the allusion to my mother as *"Jane"*, appearing as it does beside the photograph and his caption - why this particular name ? It is quite mystifying. But on studying the issue of the photographs I began to wonder. Could its use be designed to reinforce his image of a *Plain Jane* (to put it mildly) in the reader's subconscious ? I pose the question, I do not know the answer, but is there a more plausible explanation ?

8f

The 1940's and "Mrs. Gray"

What can I say about *"Mrs. Gray"* and the 1940's apart from that this entity appears to have been introduced to link the nursemaid of the Allison children, Nurse Cleaver, back to the 1909 murder trial in London, and on to further crimes of a later date ?

To explain as briefly as is possible, to those who may not be fully aware of the story. A young woman came to the public's notice in the 1940's, in America, presenting herself as Lorraine Allison, the child lost in the *Titanic* disaster along with her parents. Lorraine Kramer, as she then was, claimed to have been saved from the *Titanic* by a Mr Hyde, who brought her up and from whom she had more recently discovered her real identity. What apparently prompted her to enquire about her background was, as documented in the newspapers, the wartime requirement for non-American citizens to register as aliens.

This much the newspapers of the day reported, i.e. a Lorraine Kramer, claiming to be Lorraine Allison saved from the *Titanic*. Mr Lynch has further enlightened us that Mr Hyde was said really to be Thomas Andrews, a director of Harland and Wolff, thought to have drowned back in 1912.

I have no reason to doubt the sincerity of any of Lorraine Kramer's descendants in believing her to be Lorraine Allison. I have no personal knowledge of them which would allow me to form an opinion either way. It is just possible that she *was* one of the small children saved from the *Titanic,* were all such survivors identified ? However, it does not seem likely that Lorraine Allison would have remained unrecognised on board the *Carpathia* with the three surviving female servants of the Allison party there, plus numerous other first-class passengers who would also have recognised her.

She, and her would-be father, Mr Hyde (whoever he might be), could not have been concealed, as she is supposed to have claimed, in the doctor's cabin with Bruce Ismay (chairman and managing director of the White Star Line) for the whole voyage to New York. At the age of nearly three years she would have been able to make her presence well and truly known, the child who clung so closely to her mother is unlikely to have been quietened by a stranger. A stranger the like of Thomas Andrews would only have drawn attention to the child. He was extremely well known and respected by those on board the *Titanic,* especially the crew.

Everything is against this being possible. Bruce Ismay may have remained in the cabin throughout the journey, but nonetheless there was a steady stream of callers. Not only those looking for the doctor, but those visiting Ismay himself, including Lightoller and young Mr Thayer. The latter, as recorded in Michael Davie's book, was encouraged to do so by the doctor. From these accounts it is evident the room in question was barely large enough for the doctor and Mr Ismay. That another man and young female child could also be accommodated, appears impossible.

~~~~~

Returning to the Lorraine Kramer, who entered the public arena in the 1940's, Mr Lynch relates how, during the intervening period, she and her father Hyde had received a number of visitors. Namely, Ismay and George Allison (Hudson's brother). Both for the purpose of paying Hyde hush-money. The third visitor being

"Andrews' sister, a "Mrs. Gray." " Adding *"The revealing clue here is that "Mrs. Gray" is the same pseudonym that Alice Cleaver had invoked at her trial in 1909."*

Whether we are asked to believe in the validity of Lorraine Kramer's claim, or indeed the supposed visits by Ismay and Allison, is I feel doubtful, let us just say that the author likes to have his cake and eat it. If he doesn't think there is any truth in her claims, then can he justify repeating them and at the same time having a dig at the surviving Allison family ? If on the other hand he himself believes the story, then perhaps he should not appear to treat it with such scorn.

He further states *"It would seem more likely - from the "Mrs. Gray" connection - that it was Alice Cleaver who had supplied Loraine Kramer with Allison memories."* There is also reference to family jewellery *"sent to Bess Allison's sister who found them to be cheap imitations."*

I have commented, in an earlier chapter, on the statement made that my mother was *"hired in haste"* and corrected this to - at short notice. By use of his phrase Mr Lynch contradicts himself. In suggesting Nurse Cleaver would have had opportunity to obtain information (to provide memories relevant to the type a three-year-old child would hold of her parents), he now disregards the short time he himself stresses that she was with Bess and Hudson Allison. My mother would have needed tremendous foresight to envisage the terrible fate that was to befall many of those travelling on the *Titanic,* when she set off from Southampton on 10th April; and to have been aware of the need to obtain this information nearly thirty years in advance of its use.

Neither would she have had occasion to study Mrs Allison's jewellery. The maid would certainly have been well acquainted with the individual pieces of her lady's treasures - whose care she was responsible for - and may have handled them daily. The nurse would not.

If disbelieving of the other elements of Lorraine Kramer's story, why has Mr Lynch so readily chosen to believe that *"Mrs. Gray"* ever existed, and then linked her to my mother ? If Lorraine Kramer/Mr Hyde were able to concoct such a story in the first place, they would not have needed any help to find out a few bits and pieces about the Allisons whose situation was well documented in the newspapers.

To believe that Nurse Cleaver, using the pseudonym *"Mrs. Gray"*, assisted Lorraine Kramer, it is necessary to believe that she was associated with the 1909 murder trial, where the existence of a Mrs Gray, referred to by the defendant, was called into question. Whereas, I have shown that my mother had no connection with the 1909 trial, and therefore no connection with a Mrs Gray, whether real or imaginary. The defendant at that trial had of course died twenty-five years prior to the events now under discussion.

The supposed existence of a Mrs Gray in relation to Lorraine Kramer is therefore totally irrelevant. If by chance a woman of that name ever did frequent her life this is no great surprise - it is hardly an unusual name. But when asked where she is referred to no source for this has been forthcoming, which leaves me in severe doubt as to whether a Mrs Gray ever did exist. What is certain is that without her there would be no link, and no further charge - that of assisting in attempted extortion - could be laid against Nurse Cleaver.

This is a charge which is just as preposterous as all the others, and rests like all the others on the false assumption that my mother had a secret past, falling apart as soon as it is recognised that she did not, and was in truth a reputable children's nursemaid.

9

Deliberation and Verdict

In the light of the main charge - that of murder - the lesser charges may seem to pale. But no court of law would consider obtaining employment by deception; responsibility for the death of a family; keeping control of a baby in an attempt to afford protection and gain financial advantage; or taking part in attempted extortion, as minor charges.

That these are not allegations in a court of law, or assertions in respect of a living person, does not lessen their severity or the burden of proof.

If a public assertion of Nurse Cleaver's guilt is acceptable, then a proper examination of the evidence is the least she should be entitled to. In setting before you the true facts, this is what I have tried to do.

I have spoken of burden of proof. The prosecution has demonstrated no link between the defendant at the 1909 trial and the Allison's nursemaid, or the *Titanic*. We are just told this was so, and expected to take it for granted, as we are lack of experience in her duties, although again there is no evidence and it was clearly not the case. This, along with deception in obtaining her post, is based on nothing more than the untrue assumption that she was not a bona fide nursemaid and had a secret past. In venturing to back this up we are regaled with supposed thoughts, and accounts of what passed between her and her employers, to which only she and they were privy. In short, conjecture of the very worst kind.

The same conjecture continues as the only evidence for her actions on board both the *Titanic* and *Carpathia*, where she is said not only to bear responsibility in the death of the Allison family, but also to have held on to the child for mercenary and other unexplained reasons.

Then, the case reaches new depths as personal appearance is used against the accused. But in bringing to our attention one photograph in particular, and stating on the very same page *"her true identity remained unknown"*, the newspaper's own caption - *"Nurse Cleaver, and the little baby Allison, whom she saved from the wreck"* - is omitted.

Two of the charges - concealing her true identity and attempted extortion - are reliant on circumstantial evidence, the stated presence of *"Jane"* and *"Mrs Gray"*; having unmasked the origins of the only other evidence put forward. But even proof of the contemporary existence of these entities has not been found, or forthcoming. What sort of prosecution stamps their feet and refuses to produce to the court, when asked, the evidence and witnesses called upon to make their case ?

To assert publicly that someone is guilty, and to allow this to become true in the public perception, cannot now just be brushed aside. In a court of law the defendant faced with such severe charges would be seen to come under the scrutiny of her peers and, where justice prevails, the innocent accused, such as Nurse Cleaver, would be openly acknowledged as being just that -

Innocent of all charges.

10

The Final Judgement

This book has been partly set out in the form of a trial, because this is how I saw the attitude towards my mother from the start. Her trial nothing more than a show trial, the court nothing more than a kangaroo court. A decision having been reached without any evidence considered necessary. Readers may feel this is somewhat fanciful but my initial reaction has long been borne out.

On approaching Mr Lynch the family was expected to provide evidence of my mother, Nurse Cleaver's, innocence, whilst he has steadfastly refused to provide evidence of her guilt. So it seems she was not even to be accorded a fair trial with an independent jury, in which judgement would be made by her peers and compatriots. No, as I say, it was up to us to prove her innocence, whilst being told any evidence would be treated with scepticism. Was the person who instigated this situation to become sole arbiter, to decide whether there was any merit in our argument - without of course providing a single shred of evidence himself to show there was a case to answer ? Whatever happened to innocent until proven guilty when, ninety years after the main event, the family of someone wholly unconnected are the only ones of whom evidence is expected !

Is it too much to hope that historians should abide by the time-honoured tradition of backing up their findings and substantiating their work, and can anyone be more justified in making such a request than my mother's family ? This, after all, is the established method through which the credibility of their, and other experts, work is recognised. Where the *Titanic* is concerned fact and fiction may have long been merged, but it is not good enough to make outrageous unfounded statements about real people and then refuse to validate them.

It is ironic that those who profess to care so much about the *Titanic* and her victims (and I use the latter word in its widest sense), have been the direct means of causing so much distress. But do they *really* care ? The author has done nothing to right the dreadful wrong to my mother's memory he has perpetrated, his publishers have long since passed the buck. Hollywood has decreed that William Murdoch's name shall go down in history as a coward. It seems James Cameron's historical consultant, on that same film, would have my mother for ever identified as a convicted murderer. Doing the honourable thing, simple removal of the monstrous slurs and printing of an acceptable retraction, which would have satisfied, is ignored. We, like my mother, are treated with contempt.

~~~~~

Having discovered the truth behind the main charge, I found myself pinpointing the other charges against my mother and listing them, in order that I might investigate each one. From there noting down my thoughts, my words grew as my research progressed. Those who more fully understand the workings of the mind will appreciate this to be therapeutic, indeed it has proved to be the only way of unburdening some of the anguish.

In being forced to write this book, having explored every other reasonable avenue and found them closed, I soon became aware that it would be impossible to do so without referring to the true perpetrator of the crime. For, in order to conclusively prove my mother's innocence, it was necessary to show that the guilty party was not free to be on the *Titanic*. My concern then became not only the clearing of my mother's name, but that justice should be done to the girl who has been portrayed as an evil, scheming creature, with many of the true facts of her situation previously being withheld.

In justice to my mother, Nurse Cleaver, I have I hope abided by her wishes in maintaining her privacy, whilst at the same time proving her innocence. Those who have named my mother as a murderer will probably be the first to criticise. Some will be quick to level against me the similarly unjust charge of hypocrisy, but how lightly will I feel this charge by comparison. The girl then in prison had, by her crime, surrendered the anonymity and privacy that every law-abiding person has a right to. It is not I, but they, who plucked her from so many years obscurity and placed her on the *Titanic*, involving her with crimes and people she had never heard of, places she had never been to.

~~~~~

My book has concentrated on the work of Mr Lynch, Historian of the Titanic Historical Society, because he is the originator of these stories about my mother. But no less criticism should fall upon those who have followed in his footsteps. Those who have added to the books repeating these stories, spread my mother's name across the internet and around the world, embellishing along the way. At no time giving Nurse Cleaver's family the opportunity to refute anything being written about her. Some will no doubt hide under the excuse of Mr Lynch going before them, whilst at the same time claiming to have carried out years of their own research.

But in desecrating my mother's memory, final condemnation comes not from me. They have trespassed on and sought to damage that most fundamental bond since time immemorial - leaving no stone unturned to destroy the reputation of someone else's mother. On visiting their own mother are they proud to say what they have done ? If she is no longer alive are they uncaring as to what is said of her ?

Does the money reaped from a good story justify everything - if it is wrong to tell untruths libelling the living, how can it be right to say such things about the dead when they are no longer here to speak for themselves and protect their own good name ?

Should we have to accept that what is morally right or wrong in no way governs the behaviour of the human race at the end of the 20th century, and is it only threat of the law that affects our actions ? Taken to the ultimate conclusion, are theft and murder only wrong because there are laws against them ? If there were no laws would there be nothing left in the human psyche to deter us ?

~~~~~

And what of the Titanic Historical Society who Mr Lynch represents ? They who over the years have been quick to voice their opinions and take such a personal stance on matters concerning the victims, survivors and their families. From them not even the courtesy of a reply, and none of the assurances sought that they will respect our privacy and wishes; though their society's and officers' affairs are kept so very private.

If my mother, Nurse Cleaver, had been the one unfortunate enough to find herself so desperate, done the deed and paid for such a crime, should that in any case exclude her and her family from the compassion of the THS, or others, who are supposed to have genuine concerns for all those on board the *Titanic* ?

But if we, my mother and ourselves, were a convenient exception to the rule when she was said to be a convicted murderer, we have it seems committed a far worse crime by shattering their beliefs. Where are all their words of sympathy or compassion for us, now left in this terrible situation by virtue of one of their officers ? He stands by his work, they, in their silence, appear to condone his actions.

~~~~~

Others, grown men, from the comfort of dry land, sit in judgement on the actions of a children's nursemaid who kept her head, remained calm and saved a baby - suggesting that she should have stayed with the family, so sacrificing her own life and in the process that of the baby. Or should she just have fled like other servants, abandoning all her duties ? Should she have disobeyed her mistress's wishes, and the steward's orders, to suit the whims of strangers more than 80 years later ?

Can these really be sons of modern-day classless America who, as we enter the new millennium, retain the belief of some ancient civilization ? Should a master or mistress take with them into the next life their animals and servants, though their time is not yet up ? Such courageous thoughts from dry land, from people who would no doubt refuse to leave a sinking ship until the last rat had found a place in the lifeboats. How outspoken and brave are those sitting in judgement on people who are dead and cannot answer back. Yet even they have not the courage to reply to my mother's family.

These people have been asked to refrain from writing any more about my mother or her family, from delving any further into our lives. What right has anyone to know about the private lives of the victims - or the survivors (who chose not to benefit in any way from the horror they witnessed), if they wished to keep their lives just that - private. These were real living people, just like your own loved ones, not storybook characters. For the most part they were private individuals not celebrities. Their misfortune at being aboard the *Titanic* that awful night should not have meant they and their families were to be hounded for evermore.

In the wake of Princess Diana's death many people asked how harmless was the desire to know all about her life. I ask those who feel they have a right to know more about *Titanic* survivors, how harmless now is your wish ? There will always be those who will prey on this, claiming public interest as an excuse for intrusion. But in what other disaster of such magnitude, that 1,500 people lost their lives, would it be expected, almost demanded, that survivors and their families should come forward and bare the whole of their lives to any who want to know ?

When next you purchase a plane, train or boat ticket do you agree to every detail of your life becoming the property of others, and do you also sign away the rights of your children and grand-children to privacy ? What could be our excuse for wishing to know about the victims of Lockerbie, or the survivors of the Kings Cross fire and the *Herald of Free Enterprise* sinking ? Yet, in the case of the former, already their names and details are starting to be published. Are their private lives to be opened to the world and then to be judged as well ?

~~~~~

I started my book with a quote from Omar Khayyam the astronomer poet of Persia, true *Titanic* buffs will know the significance of his name to the 1912 disaster. I end with observations of my own:-

Beware of those who now jump to use mistaken identity as an excuse. Who now clutch at straws trying to suggest that my mother was ever mistaken for a woman who died nearly 85 years ago. But mistaken identity does not come into it. They relied on material against which no specific sources are cited, despite there being nothing to prevent them from undertaking the obligatory research.

Beware of those who now, contrary to the family's wishes, rush to print *any* of my mother's or our own details. Using the fact that they have so shamefully drawn a private individual into the public light as an excuse to publish these.   If sadly this does prove to be the case then I will wonder why they did not see fit to put their research skills into action a great deal earlier, establishing the truth before such lies were written.

These are no respecters of Nurse Cleaver's or other *Titanic* survivors' wishes. All the family have ever asked for is withdrawal of the lies and in their stead a simple acceptable apology to my mother. If this were your relative, falsely stated to be a convicted murderer, amongst the many other charges, would you think it unreasonable, or too much to expect ?

I ask that if you care, really care at all, about those on the *Titanic* you will support me in my endeavour to allow my mother, Nurse Cleaver, to rest in peace, her reputation restored and her family to recover from the terrible nightmare visited upon us.

Acknowledgements

I would like to thank the Public Record Office, for being the primary means of proving my mother's innocence. The British Library for its vast newspaper and periodical collection, which has yielded the extracts reproduced in this book, and from which much valuable knowledge has been gleaned. Plus the Metropolitan, and numerous other archives and libraries, in and around London, that provide such a rich source of information and assistance. I hope the staff of the many repositories concerned will forgive me for not naming their own individually, but to attempt to do so would be to risk unintentional omission.

I would like to express my gratitude to Mr Richard J Johnson of Aylesbury for allowing use of his excellent period photographs of Aylesbury Prison - one of which features on the front cover.

Main Public Record Office documents utilized in Chapters 4 and 6 include:-
CRIM 1/112/1; CRIM 1/583, no 45; CRIM 4/1287, Mar 1909; CRIM 5/9;
CRIM 6/22, 60, 80; CRIM 6/22, 8-9 Mar 1909; HO 46/176, 182, 191;
HO 140/274, p 16; HO 144/1034/176577; HO 163/42-77;
HO 163/42, pp 448-449; HO 163/58, p 709; HO 163/67, p 964
Specific quotations:-

Page	22	CRIM 1/112/1, p 72	Page	36	CRIM 1/583, no 45
"	37	HO 163/42, pp 448-449	"	46	HO 163/58, p 709
"	46	HO 144/1034/176577, no 7, Mar 1909 witness examinations, Leary			
"	49	HO 144/1034/176577, no 2, Mar 1909 Phillimore to Home Office			
"	51	HO 163/67, p 964			
"	52	HO 144/1034/176577, no 27, Oct 1914 Medical Officer's report			
"	52	HO 144/1034/176577, no 27, Jan 1915 Duchess of Bedford to Dryhurst			
"	54	CRIM 1/112/1, p 23			

Cover Illustrations

Front -   Justice with her scales, the Old Bailey
                 Aylesbury Prison (see above)
                 RMS *Titanic, New York Times,* 28th April 1912
Back -   Above the main entrance of the Old Bailey
                 Rhyme from *The Eagle,* off the City Road
                 Trinity Hospice, Clapham Common

Bibliography

Michael Davie, *The Titanic:The Full Story of a Tragedy*
(The Bodley Head, London, 1986)

Washington Dodge, *The Loss of the Titanic*
(Published by the Author, 1912)

Archibald Gracie, *Titanic, A Survivor's Story*
(Sutton Publishing, Gloucestershire, 1985)
(First published as *The Truth about the Titanic*, 1913)

Donald Hyslop, Alastair Forsyth & Sheila Jemima,
Titanic Voices: Memories from the Fateful Voyage
(Sutton Publishing, Gloucestershire, 1997)
(First published by Southampton City Council)

Walter Lord, *A Night to Remember*
(Henry Holt and Company, New York, 1955)
(Longmans, Green and Co., London, 1956)

Don Lynch & Ken Marschall, *Titanic: An Illustrated History*
(Hodder & Stoughton, London, 1992; paperback edition 1998)

The Story of the Titanic as Told by Its Survivors -
Lawrence Beesley   - *The Loss of the S.S. Titanic,*
                            Its Story and Its Lessons
Archibald Gracie   - *The Truth about the Titanic*
Commander Lightoller   - *Titanic*
Harold Bride   - *Thrilling Tale by Titanic's Surviving*
                            Wireless Man
Edited by Jack Winocour
(Dover Publications, New York, 1960)

Ben Weinreb and Christopher Hibbert, *The London Encyclopedia*
(Macmillan, London, 1983)

She Would Not Leave Husband and Went Down with Titanic.

MRS. H. J. ALLISON

CHOOSES TO DIE WITH HUSBAND

Woman Defies Command of Titanic Officer to Get Into Lifeboat.

DAUGHTER PERISHES, TOO

Milwaukee Relative Is Told Story of Tragic Fate of the Allison Family.

Milwaukee, Wis., April 19.—[Special.]—Thrilling as were many of the terribly pathetic tales which came from the lost Titanic, none was more pitiful or tragic than that related today by long distance telephone from New York to Mrs. Adam Gross of Milwaukee by her niece of the death of Mrs. H. J. Allison of Ontario by the side of the husband she refused to leave.

With Mrs. Allison and her husband died their little daughter, Lorraine, but as the last boat pushed off from the Titanic, Mrs. Allison forced her sister, Miss Sadie Daniels, to take her 7 months' son, Wilbur, and escape. Miss Daniels, although stunned by the terrible sights she had witnessed, was able to tell connectedly, even graphically, the story of the devotion of Mrs. Allison to her husband.

Refused to Leave Husband.

Here is the story as she told it to Mrs. Gross:

"Sister died rather than leave her husband, when the officers refused to let both into the lifeboat. She said life was not worth living alone and she went down even smiling, with her arm around Herbert.

"When the boat struck few realised there was any danger. Herbert and Bessie laughed and went back to dress. When we stood together at the rail, as the boats were being sent away, I was standing with Wilbur, and Lorraine was with Herbert and Bessie. Then came the order 'Women only,' and an officer tried to put Bessie in the boats.

"'Not without my husband,' she cried. 'You must,' cried the officer, but Bessie threw her arms around Herbert's neck and refused to leave him. Then after the officer stopped trying to force her into the boat she ran to me, pushed me into the boat, and threw little Wilbur after me.

No Room for Little Girl.

"The boat was full, and she grasped Lorraine with one arm, and her husband with the other, and stood waving her hand, and, it seemed to me, smiling, as she saw us rowing away. The last I saw, just as the boat started to plunge to the bottom, was Bessie turning to her husband for a farewell kiss, as the water washed to their knees. Lorraine was holding to her mother's skirts."

SAYS MOTHER FORCED PERJURY IN EVIDENCE AGAINST FATHER.

Girl's Story About to Lead to Indictment When She Breaks Down and Accuses Parent.

There appeared nothing for the Criminal court grand jury to do yesterday in the case of Jacob Trapp, 3901 North Herndon street, but indict him on a serious charge, when his 11 year old daughter, Margaret, chief witness against him, started to cry at the close of her testimony. Assistant State's Attorney Roy Fairbank asked the girl aside and asked her why she was crying. She then sobbed out that she had perjured herself by order of

PERIL ON LAKE SHIPS SHOWN

Few Vessels Going Out of Chicago Have Enough Lifeboats.

SAY THEY OBEY THE LAWS.

Owners Insist They Carry What Government Requires.

Investigation yesterday failed to disclose a single Chicago company engaged in lake transportation whose officials would say their patrons were safeguarded by a sufficient number of lifeboats and rafts to accommodate a full passenger list.

Inquiries as to the lifeboat equipment of some of the lake lines were met with by evasive answers and refusals to discuss the matter. Others talked frankly and said they regarded it unnecessary to carry lifeboats enough to empty the vessels of all passengers

total life saving capacity of 1,944 cubic feet, sufficient for 300 persons; regular passenger list, 480 life preservers, 2,172; four cork ring buoys; eight life boats lowered in one minute and thirty-five seconds; thirteen streams for water for fire in same time. Last May this vessel carried 3,186 people. June, 7,030; July, 7,316; August, 6,071; September, 2,022, showing that in case of trouble life saving equipment probably would have been sufficient

CITY OF CHICAGO—Graham and Morton line, St. Joe, Mich.; steel; 1,200 excursion capacity, including crew of about fifty; regular passenger list of about 500; four bulkheads, five metallic life boats, three rafts, one excursion boat, with total life saving capacity of 2,066 cubic feet, or sufficient for about 210 people, four cork buoys, 2,559 life preservers, six boats lowered in forty seconds at last fire drill, fourteen streams of water thrown in thirty-five seconds, same drill.

City of Benton Harbor.

CITY OF BENTON HARBOR—Graham & Morton line; St. Joe, Mich.; steel; regular passenger capacity, 613; four water-tight bulkheads, eight metallic lifeboats, two rafts, with total life saving capacity of 1,513 cubic feet, or sufficient space in boats and on rafts for 152 persons; 3,758 life preservers, six cork buoys; all boats lowered in one and one-half minutes at last inspection; fifteen streams of water thrown in 25 seconds, same drill.

HOLLAND—Graham & Morton line; 1,397 excursion capacity, including crew of about 50, 3 cross bulkheads; 8 metallic lifeboats, 4 rafts, 5 cork buoys, with total life saving capacity of 1,556 cubic feet, or about 180 people; regular passenger list,

CITY MOURNS TITANIC DEAD

Many Memorial Services Tomorrow; Will Swell Relief Fund.

MINISTERS TAKE UP MOVE.

Sermons Will Draw Lessons from Disaster; Union Meeting on North Side.

Scarce a Chicago minister will leave the topic of the Titanic disaster out of his sermon tomorrow. Since the news of the sinking of the great liner came the clergymen of Chicago have been planning memorial services and preparing special sermons on the subject.

One of the large memorial services will be held at the Episcopal cathedral of SS. Peter and Paul, Washington boulevard and Peoria street. Dean Sumner will preach on the story of the Titanic. An invitation has been taken by Dean Sumner to the office forces of the White Star line, the Cunard line, and

WIRELESS ON BOATS FAULTY

Chicago Operators Criticise Lake and Ocean Equipments.

TELL WHY TITANIC'S FAILED.

Urge Storage Batteries Instead of Dynamo for Power.

Wireless equipment on ocean steamships and on lake passenger boats sailing from Chicago was called antiquated and inadequate last night at a meeting of the Chicago Wireless association at 36 East Van Buren street. It was stated that the power for the wireless on these boats is, with one exception, furnished by dynamos. When the dynamo stops the wireless is useless.

The amateur operators asserted during the discussion that the power for the wireless should be furnished by storage batteries which are not so likely to fail.

"Sometimes when the operator wants to